I0468157

Introduction

Within the pages of this book you will find a variety of different species of birds from around the world for your own colouring creativity.

Simply relax, de-stress yourself and use your own imagination when colouring in these wonderful designs.

Why not share your completed designs with others?

You can also share your completed designs with others on our Facebook page below, where you will also find more free colouring designs and patterns for you to colour in.

https://www.facebook.com/Best-Adult-Coloring-Books-1497039227284351/

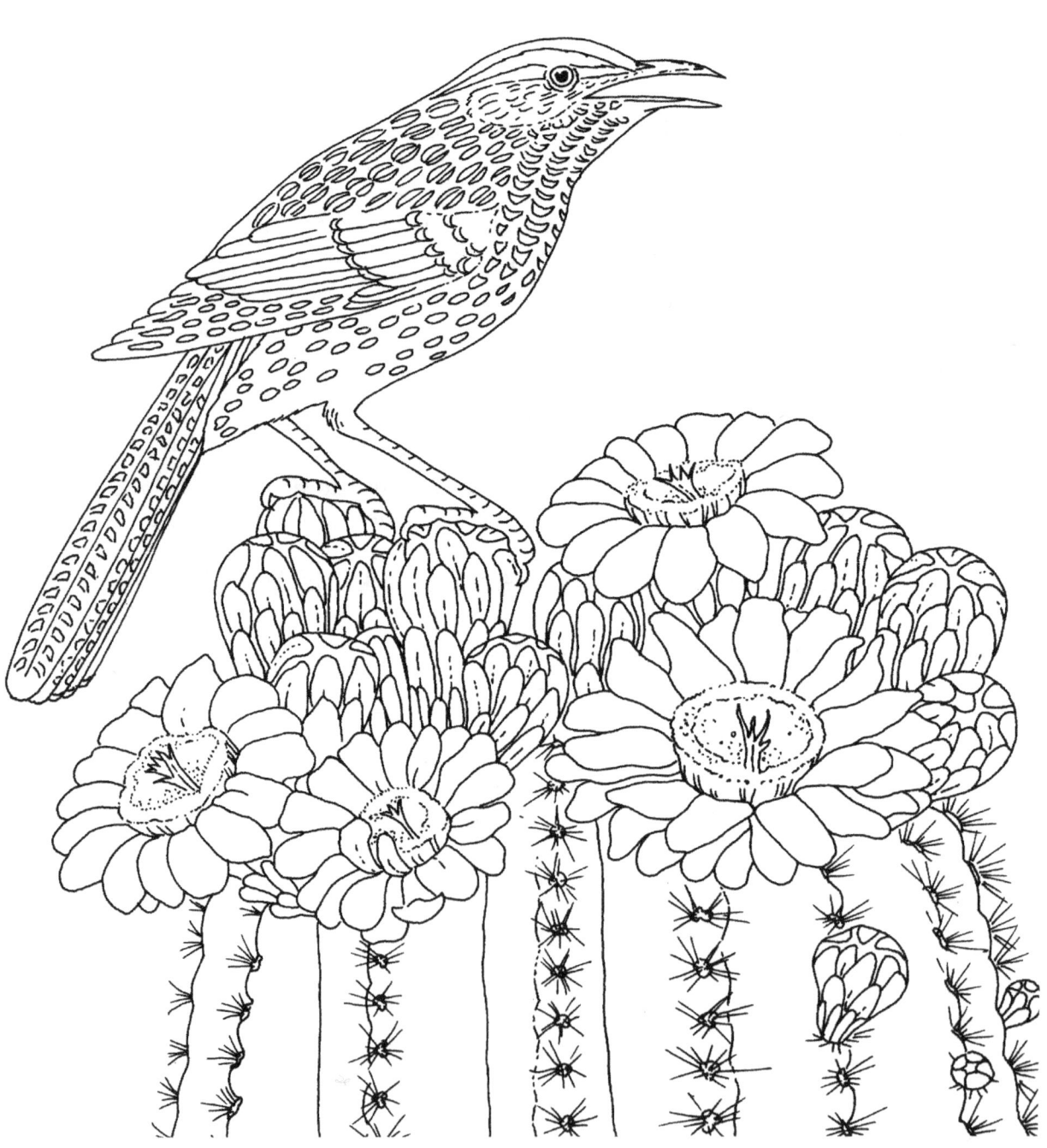

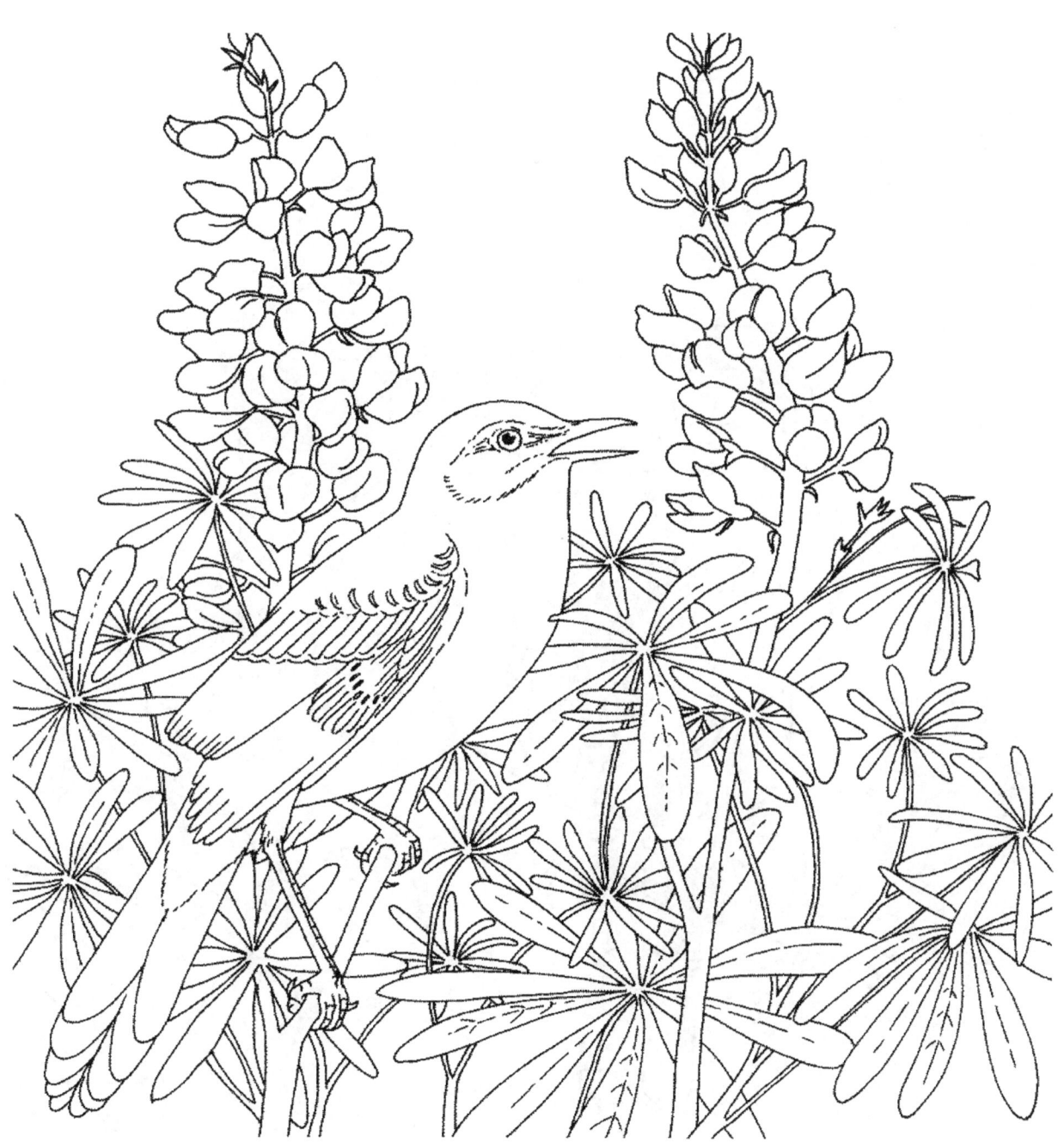

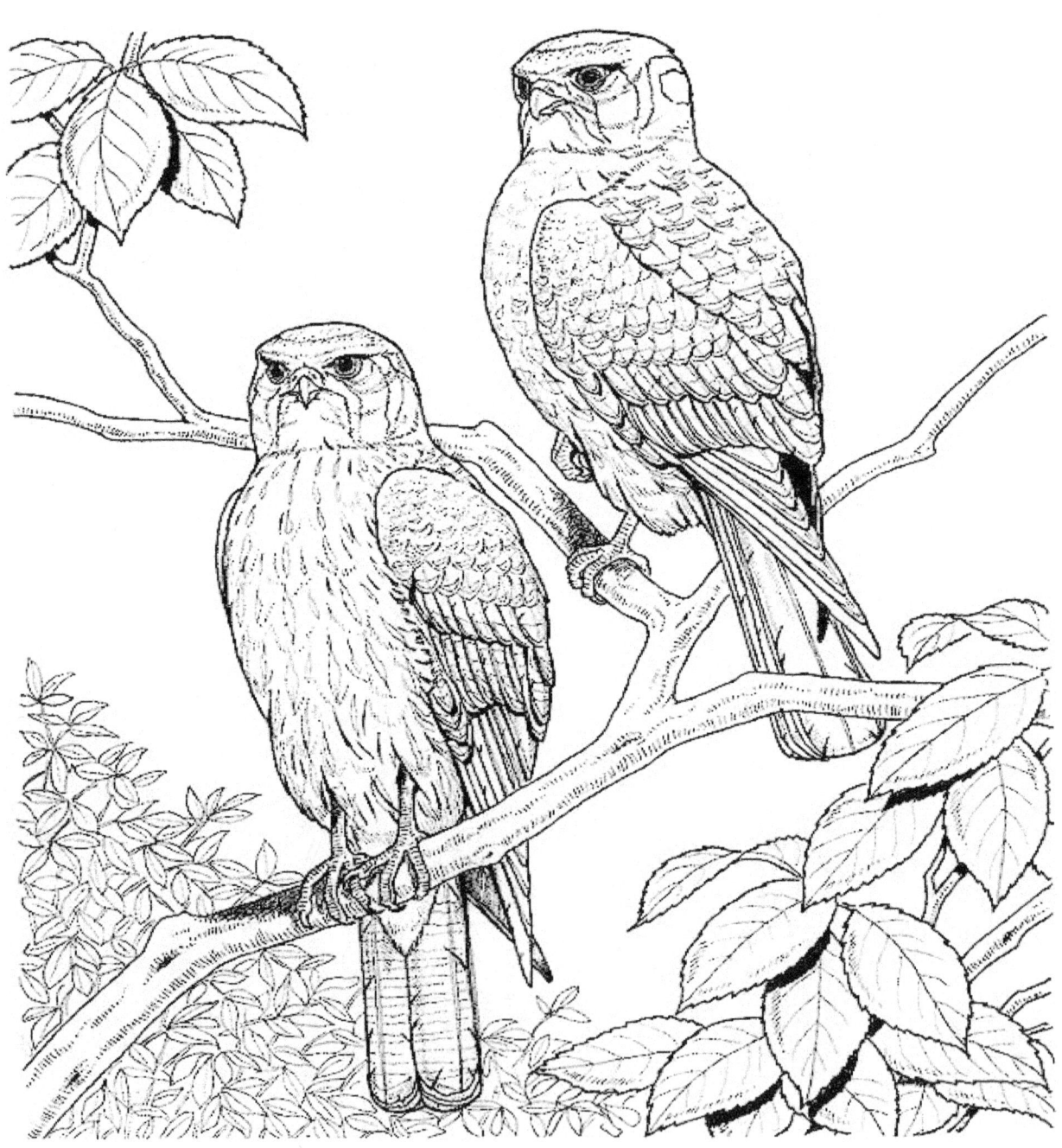

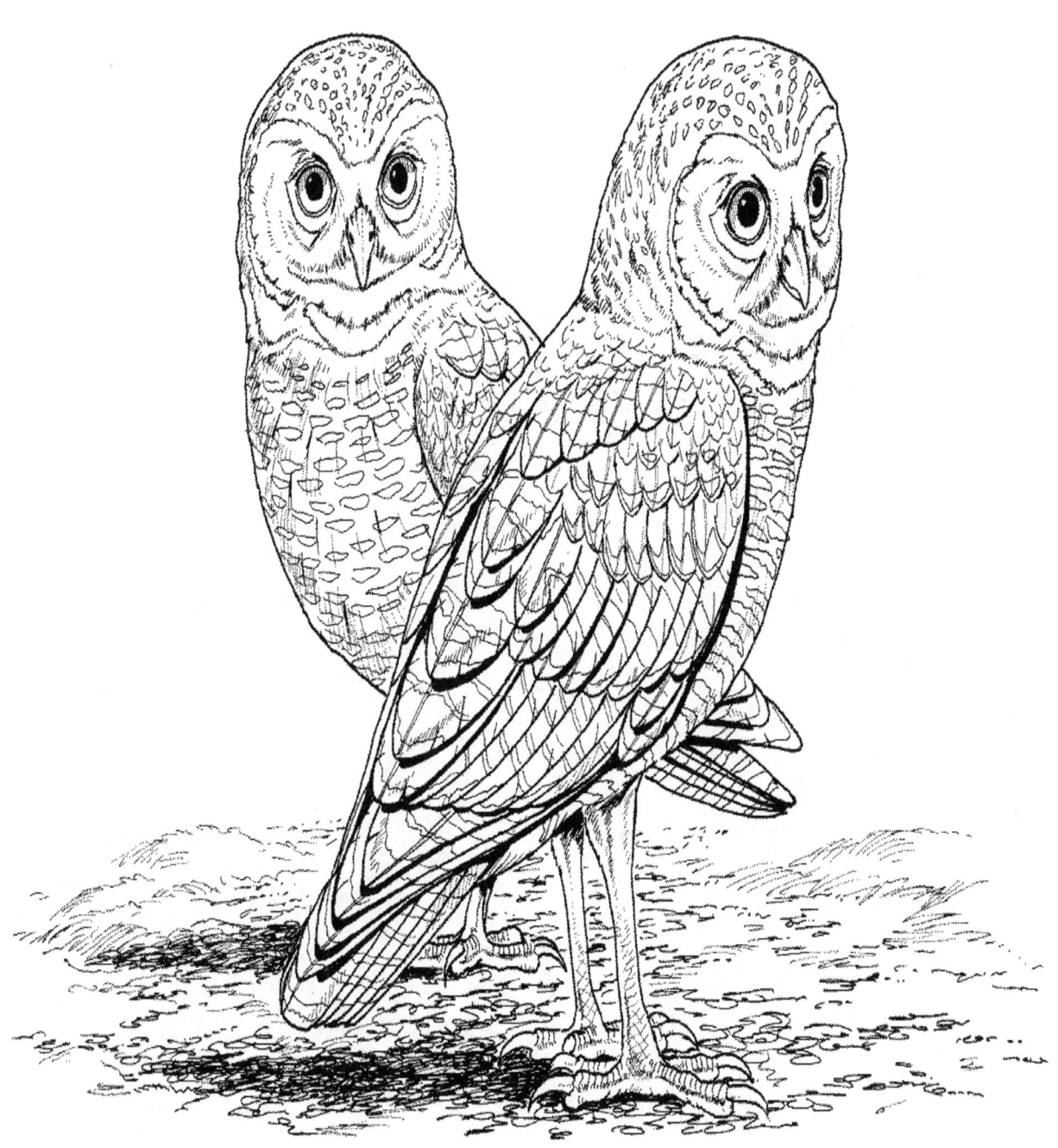

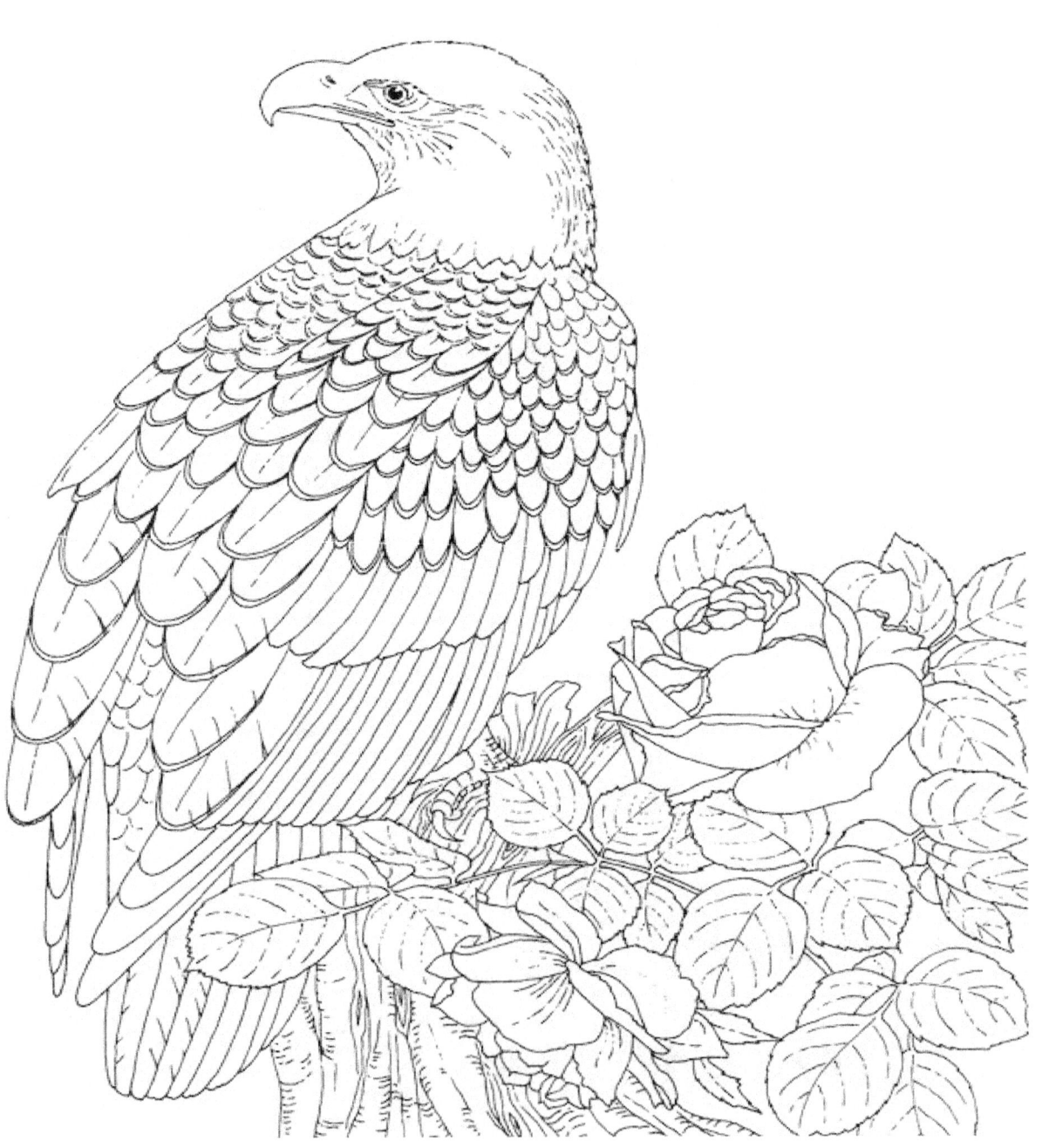

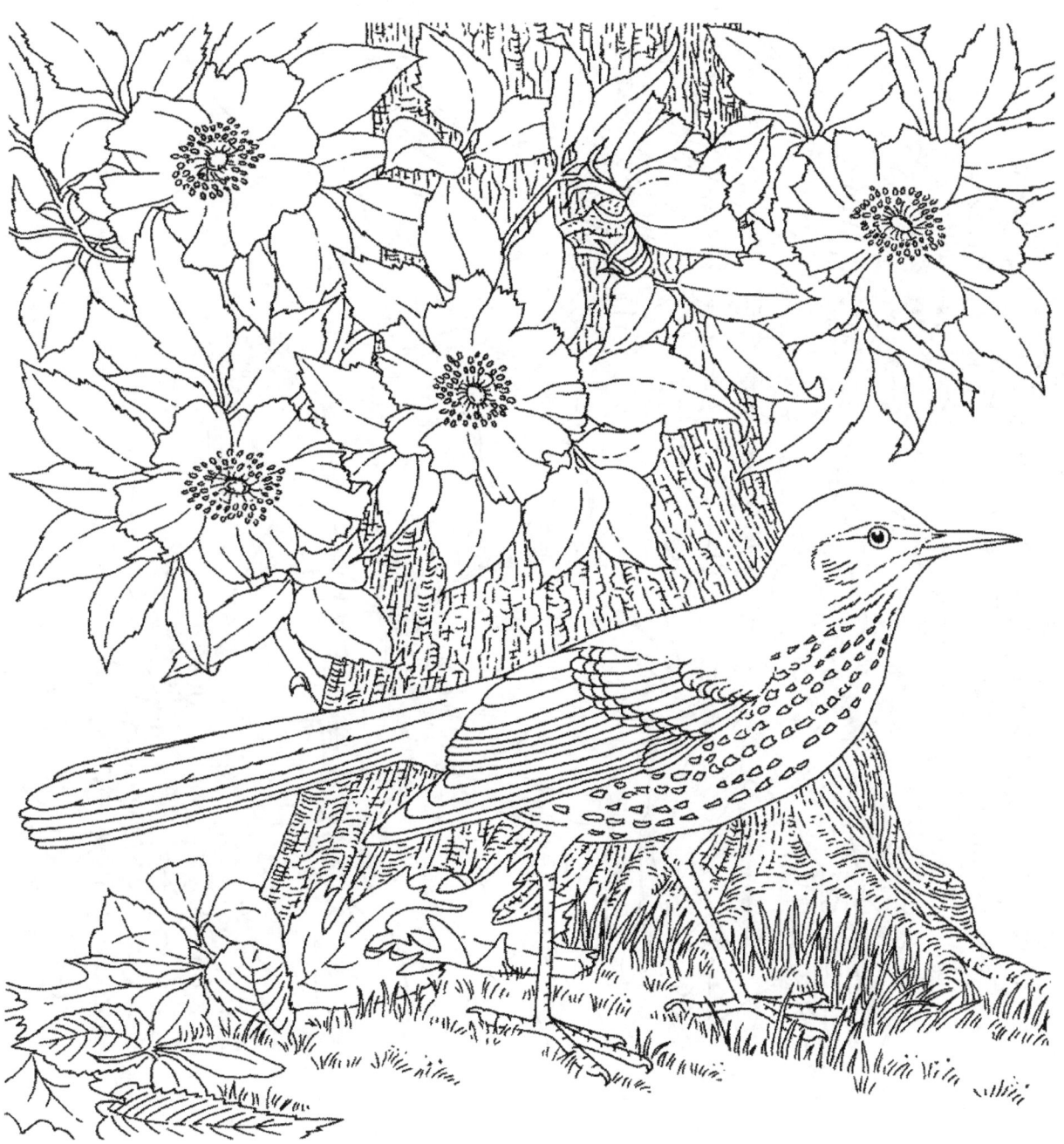

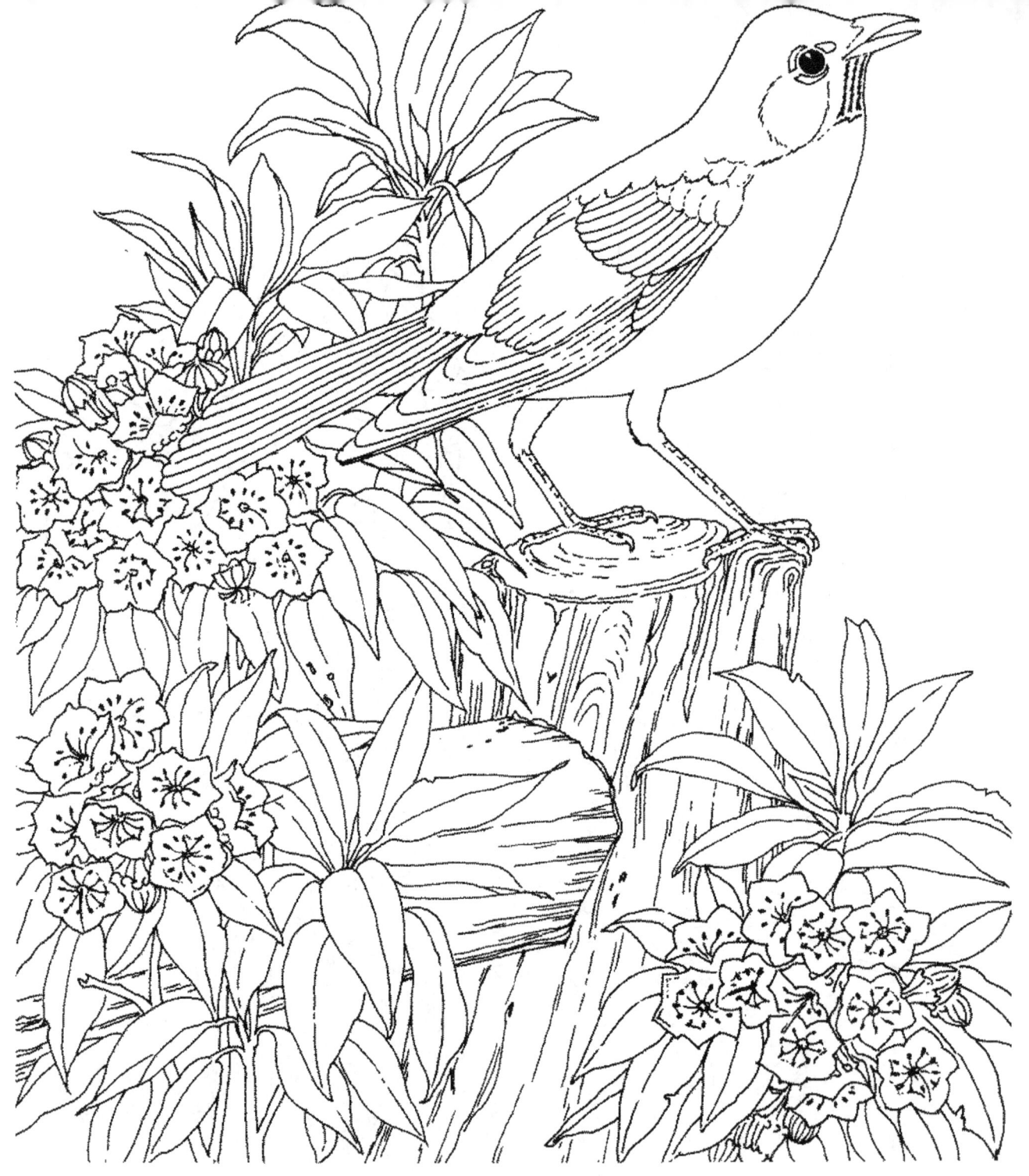

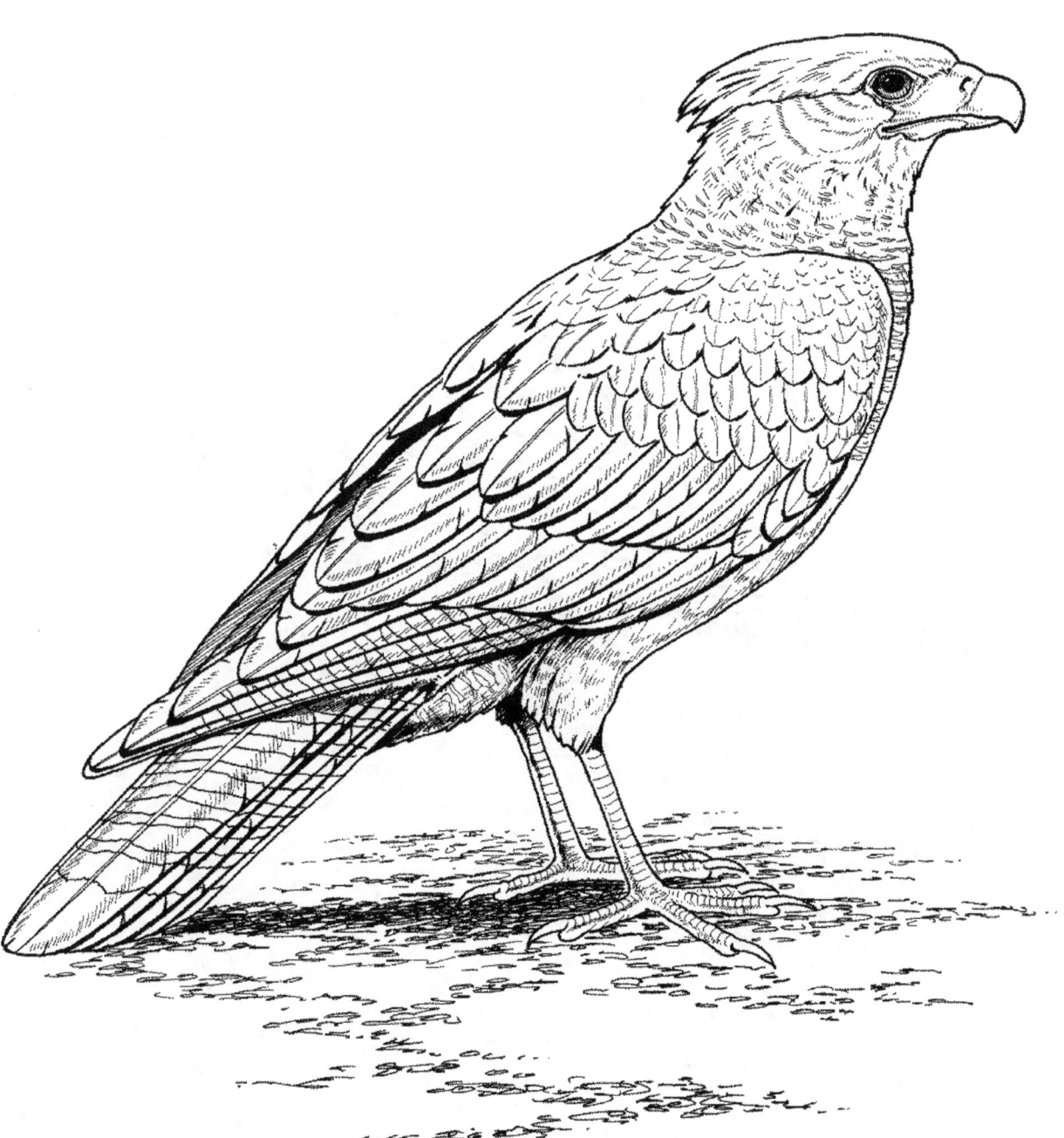

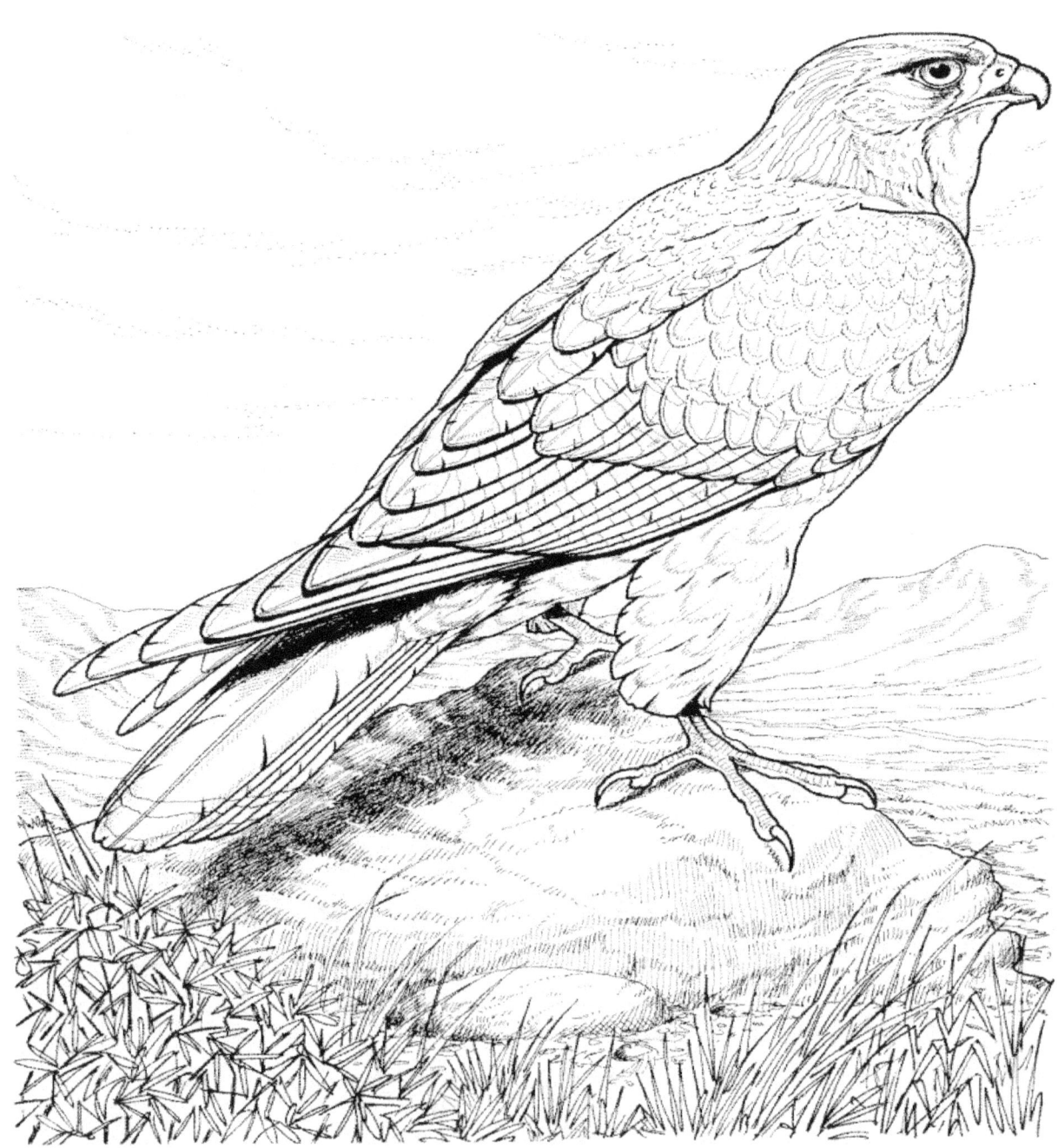

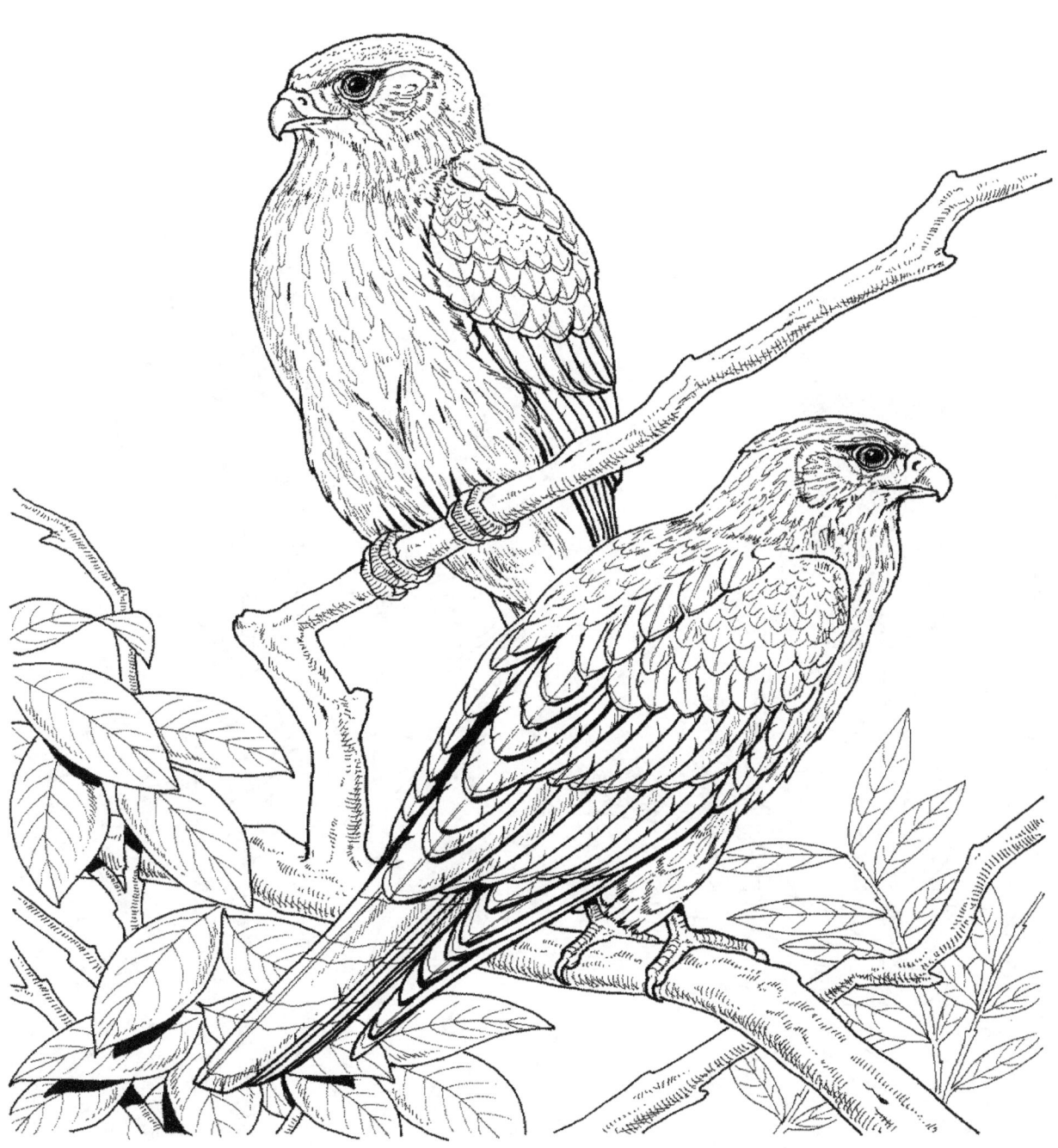

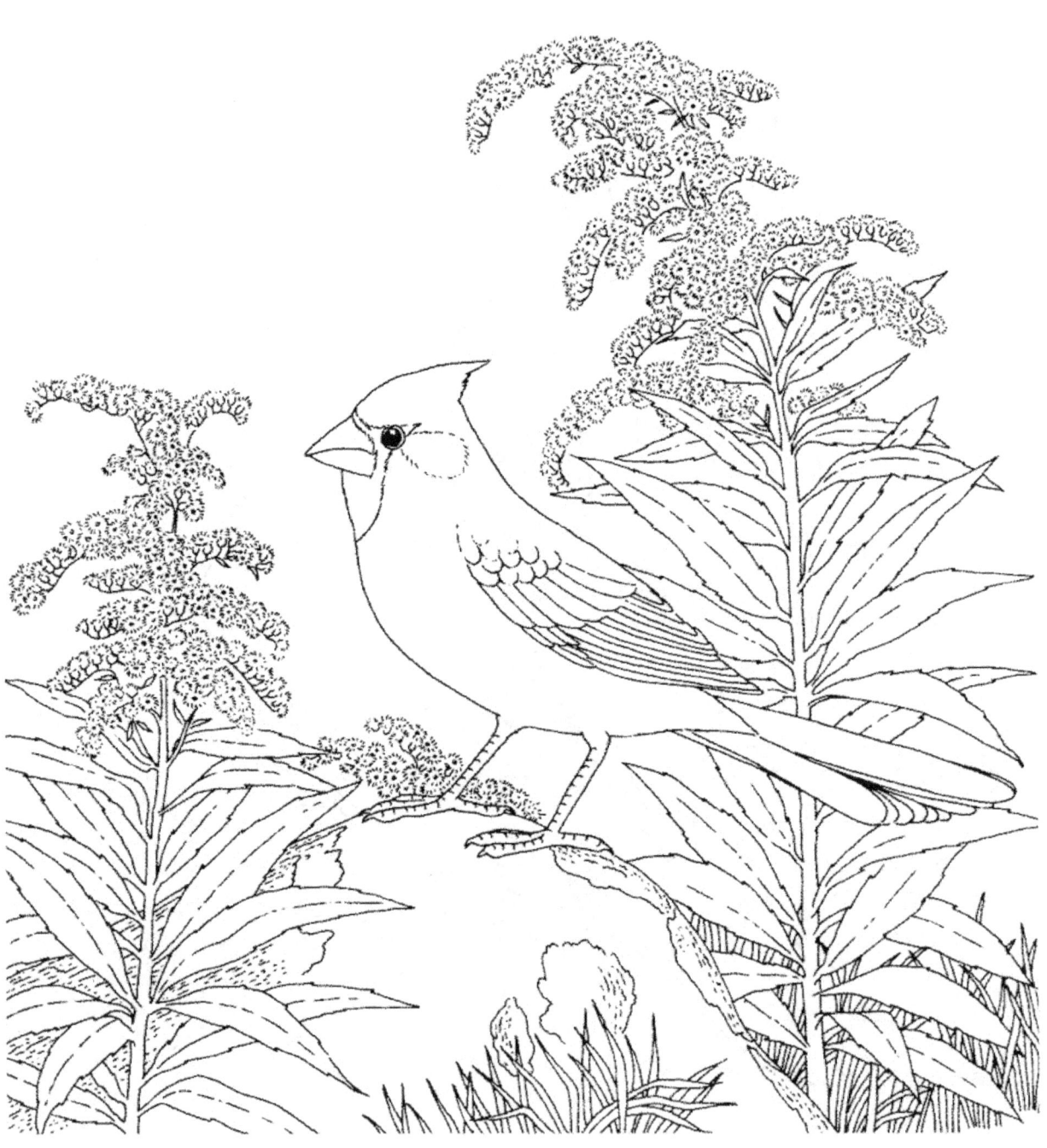

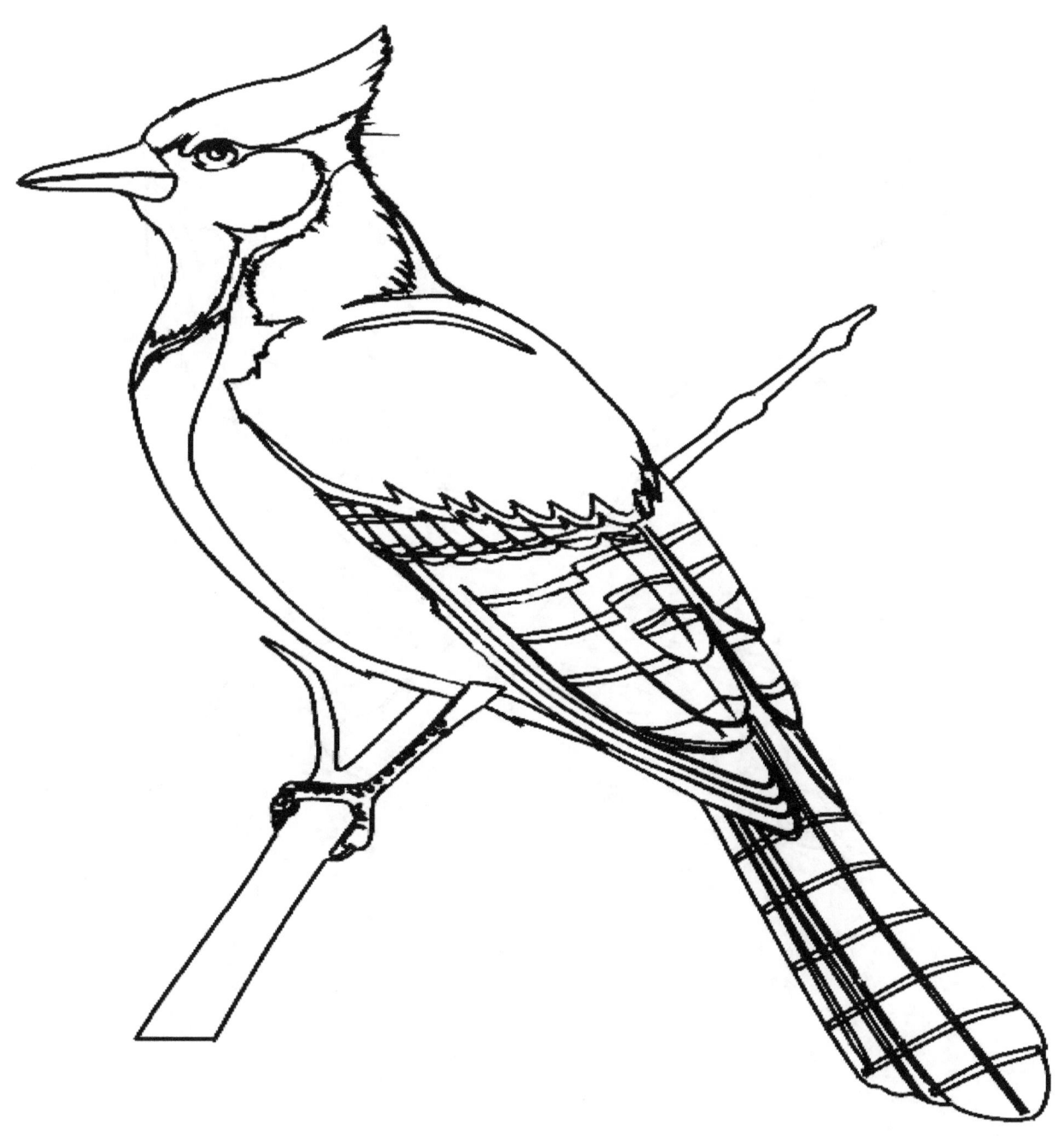

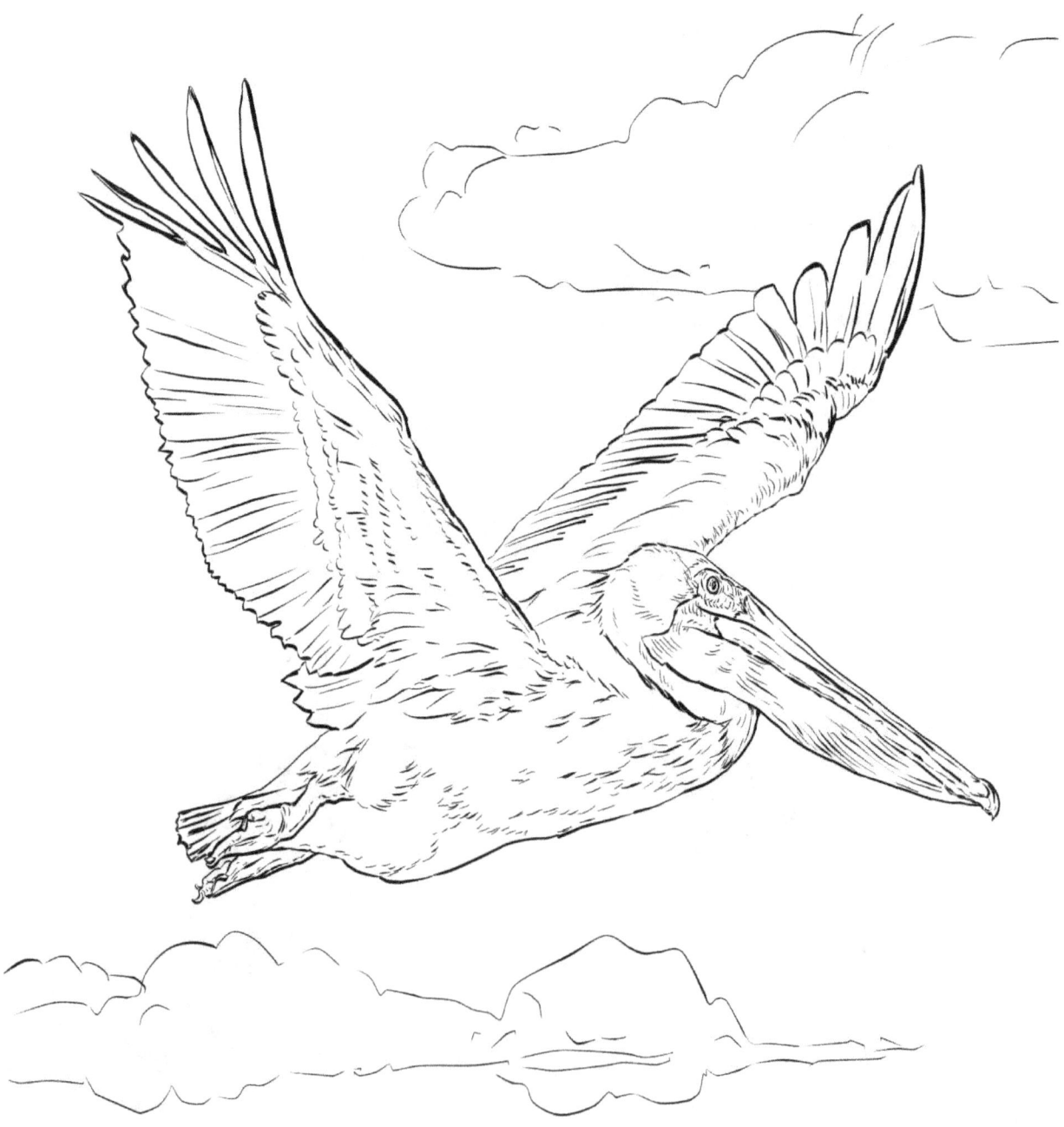

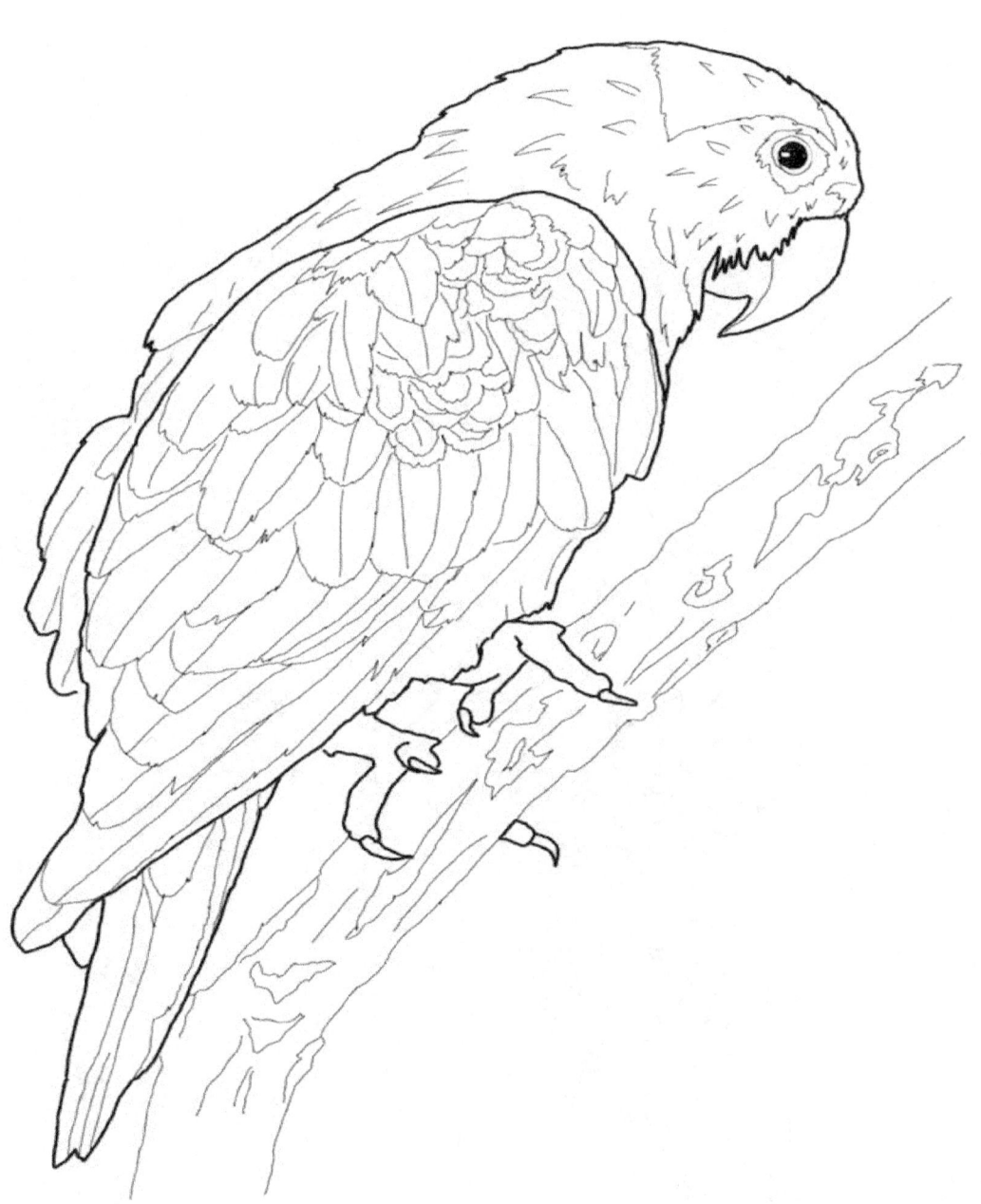

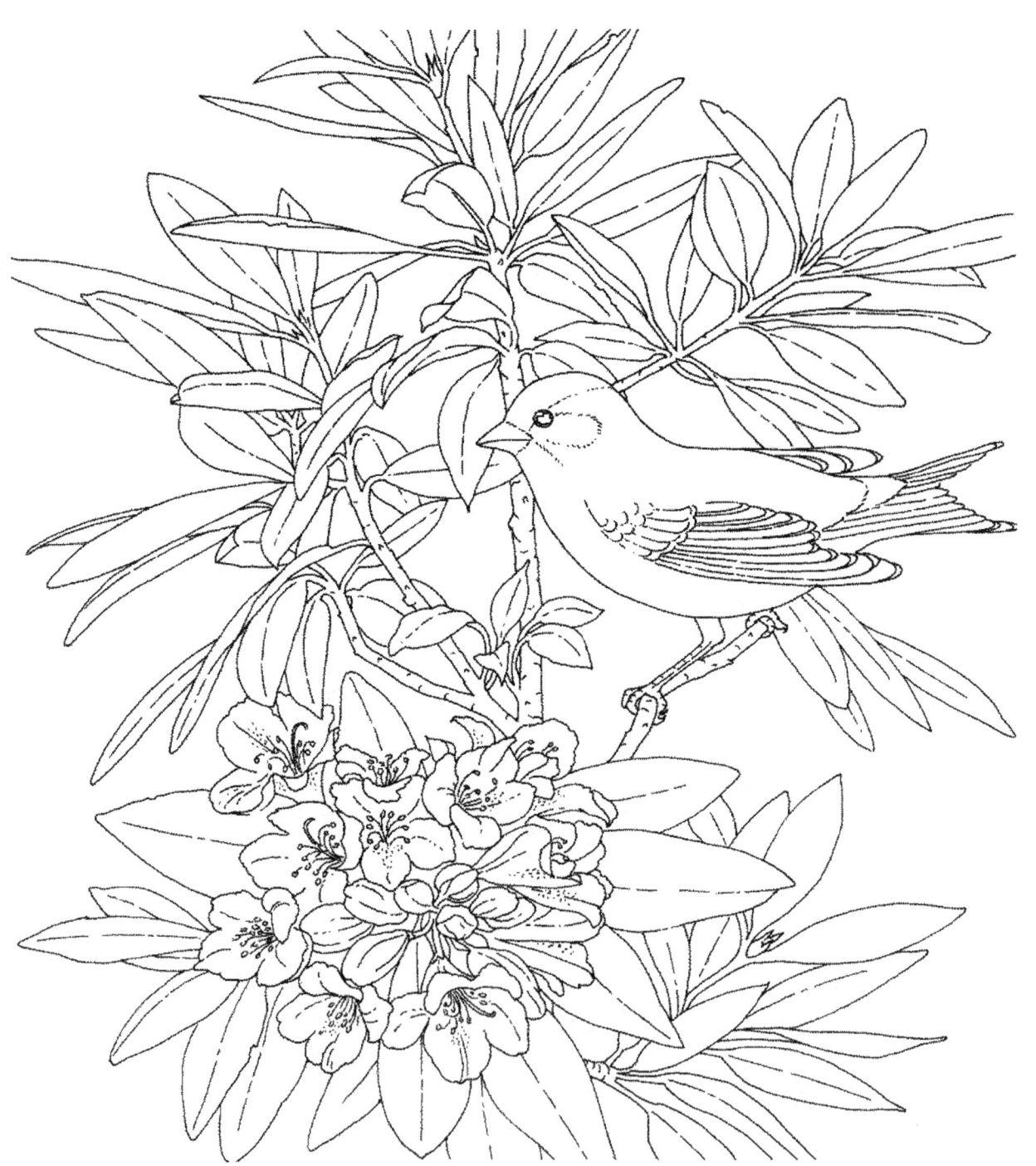

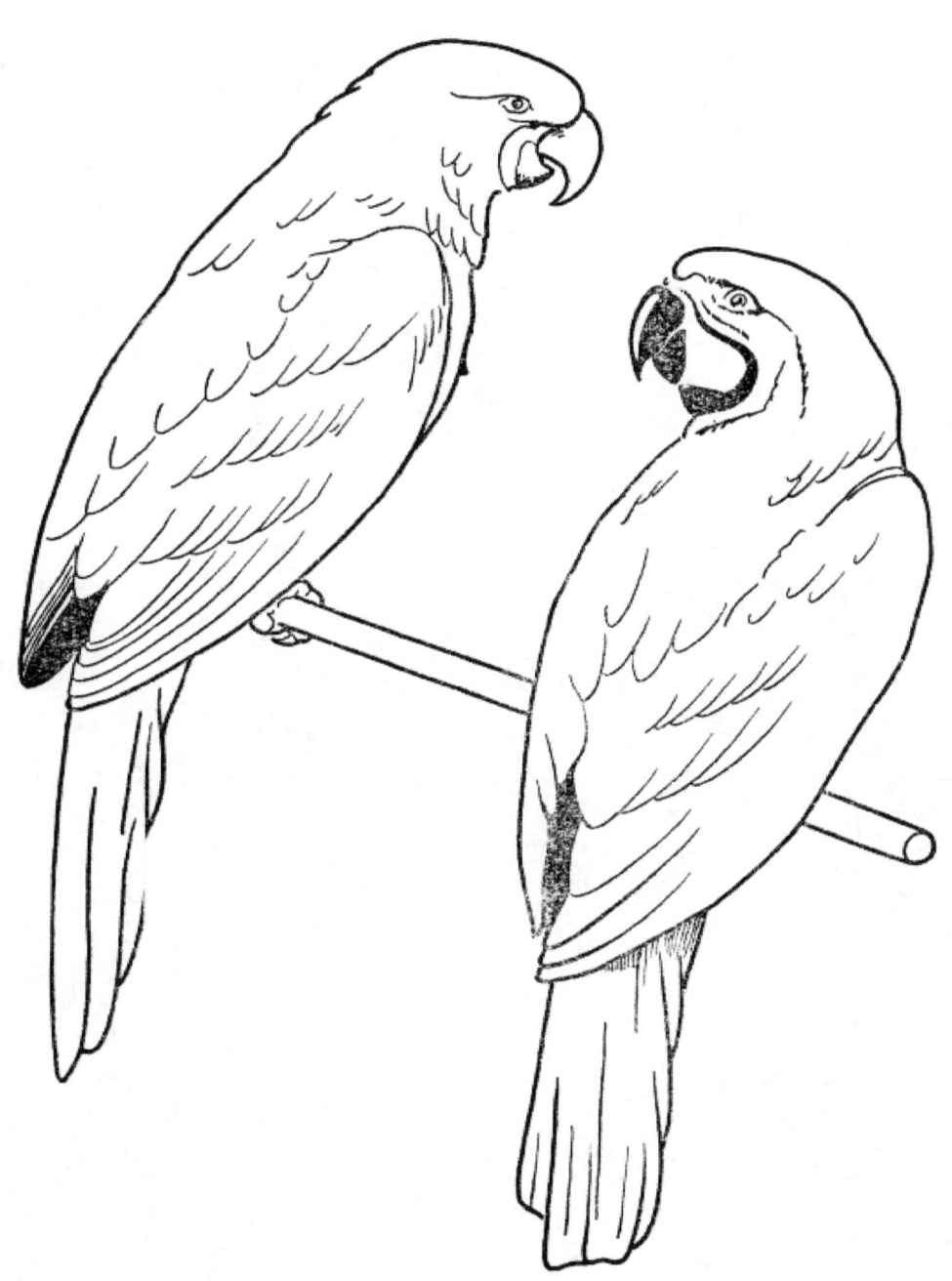

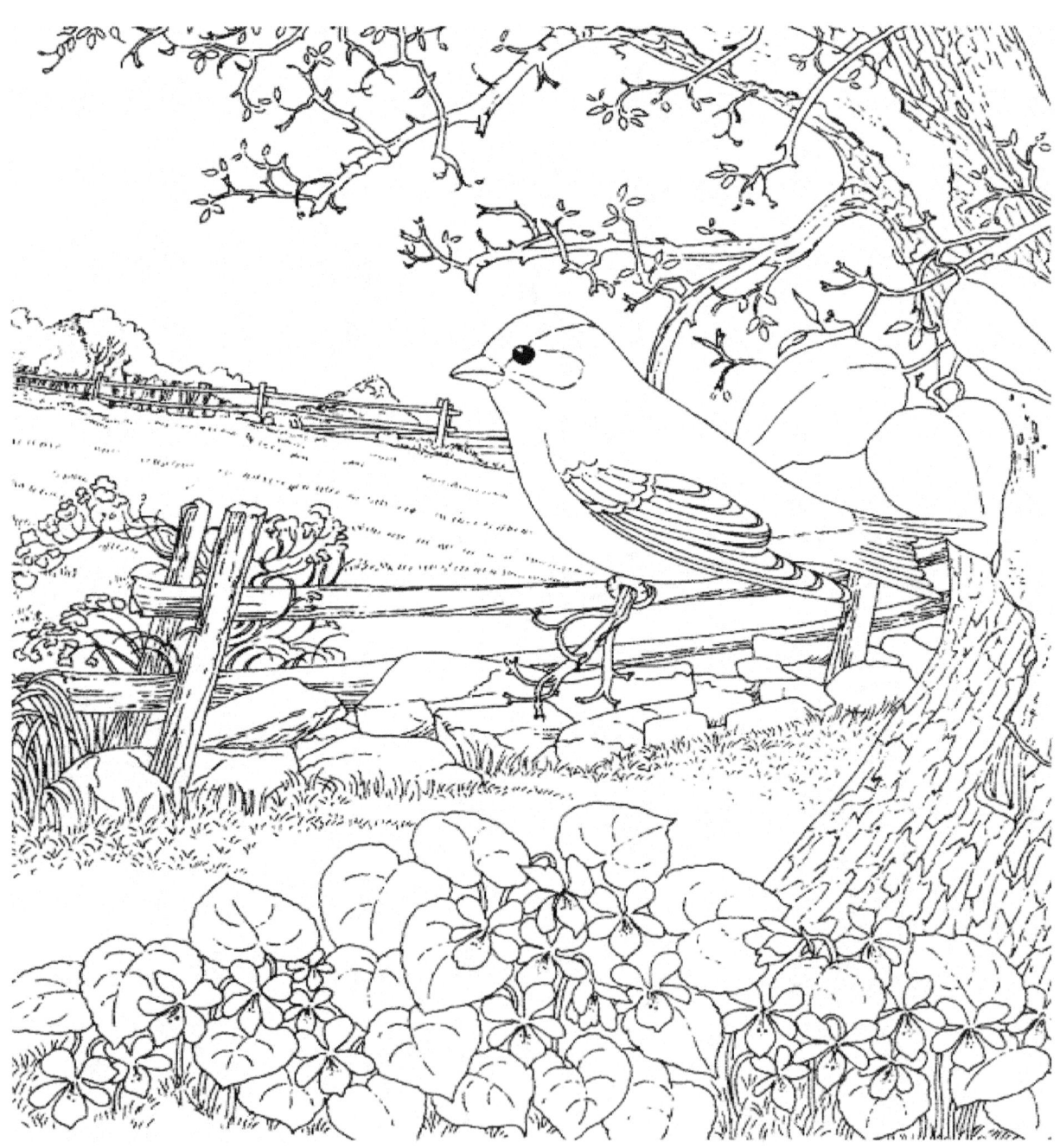

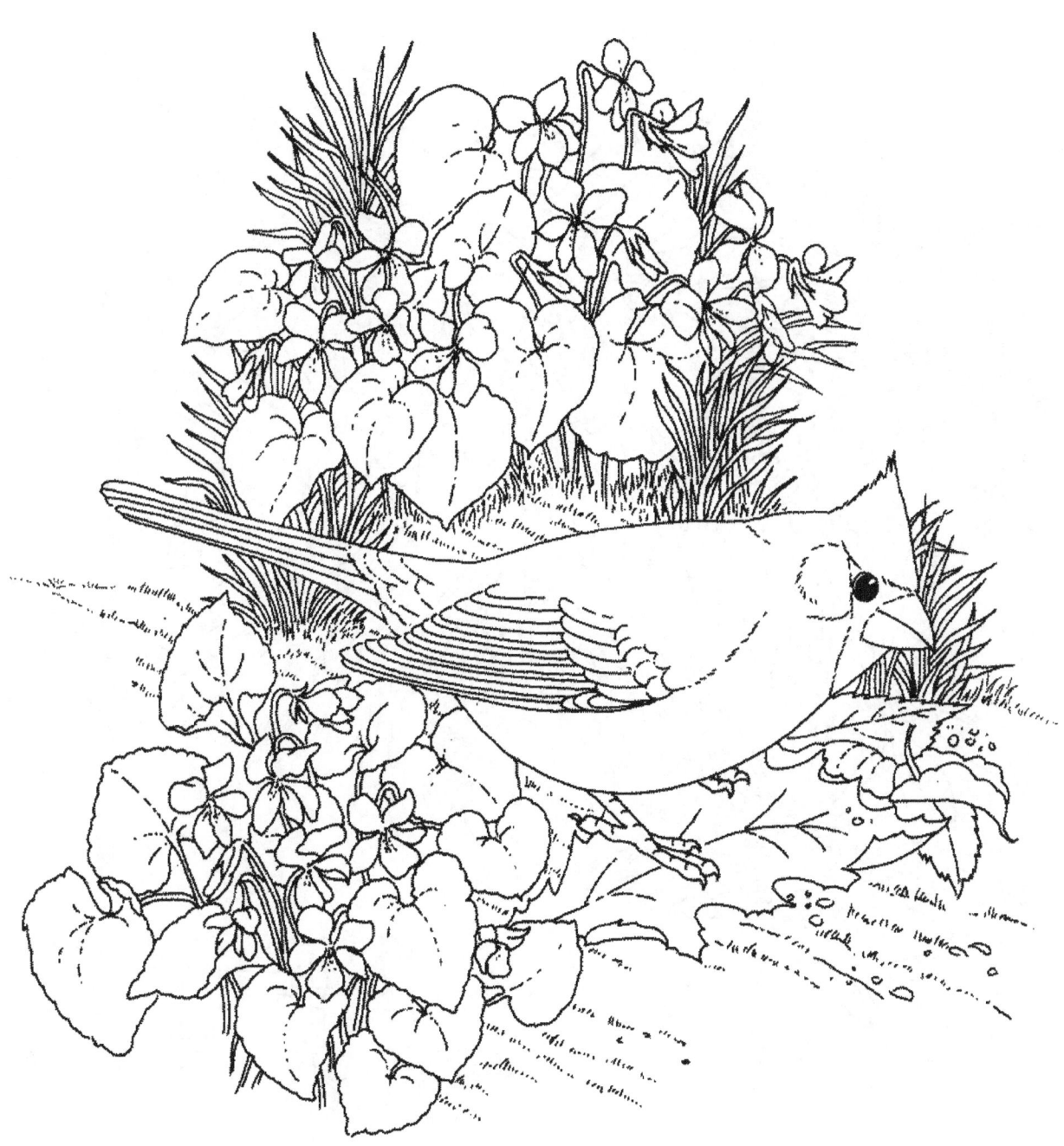

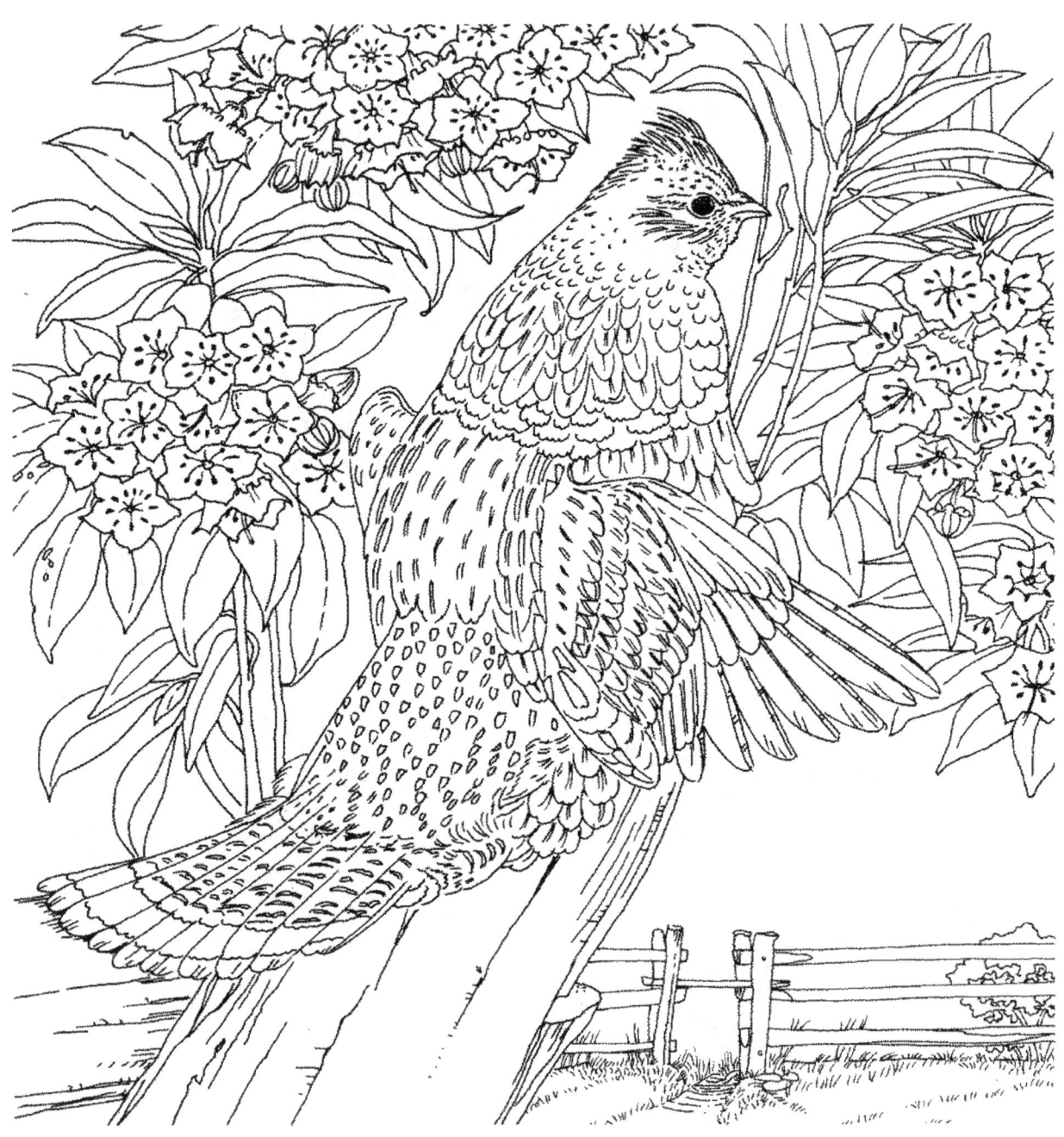

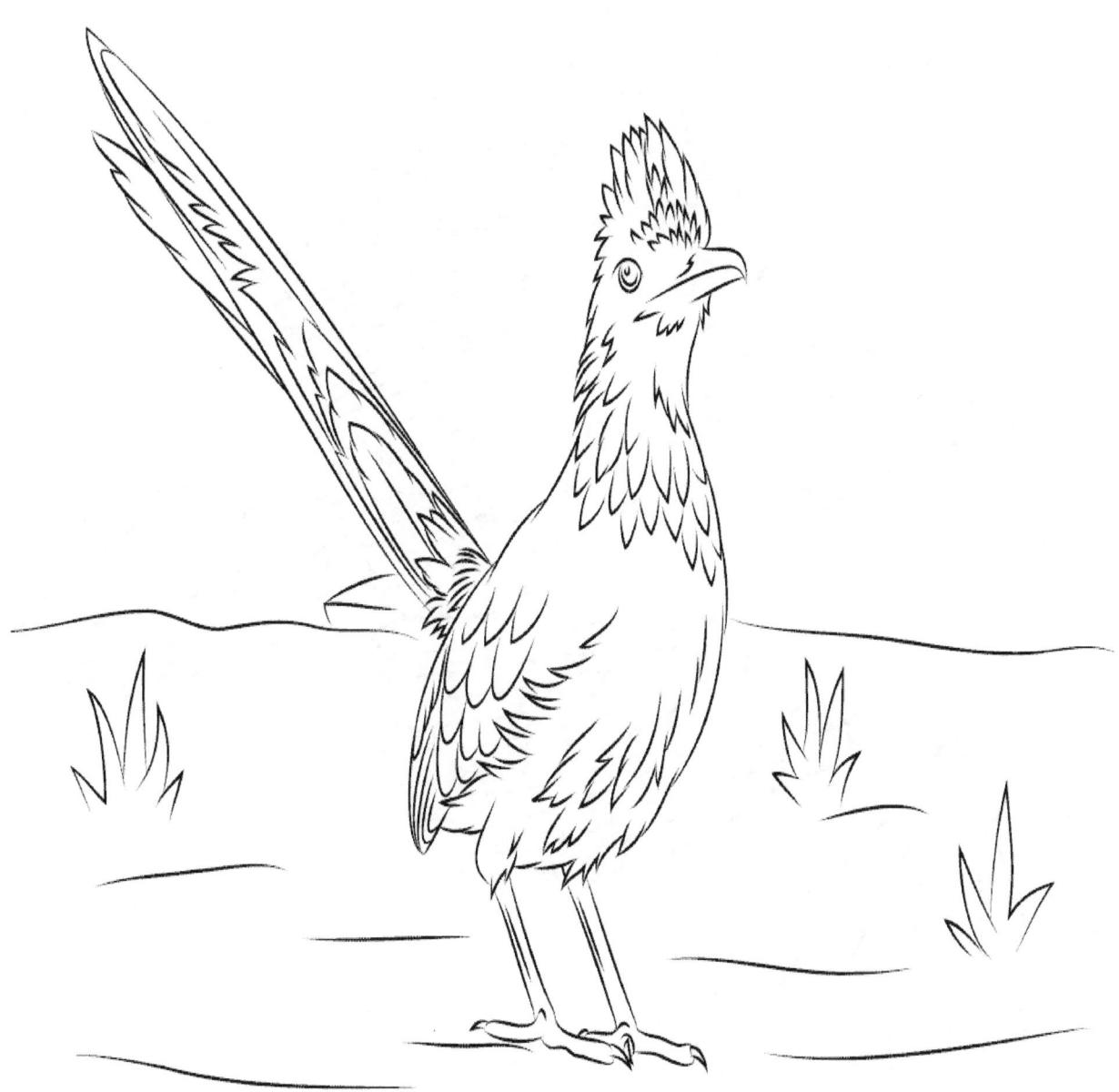

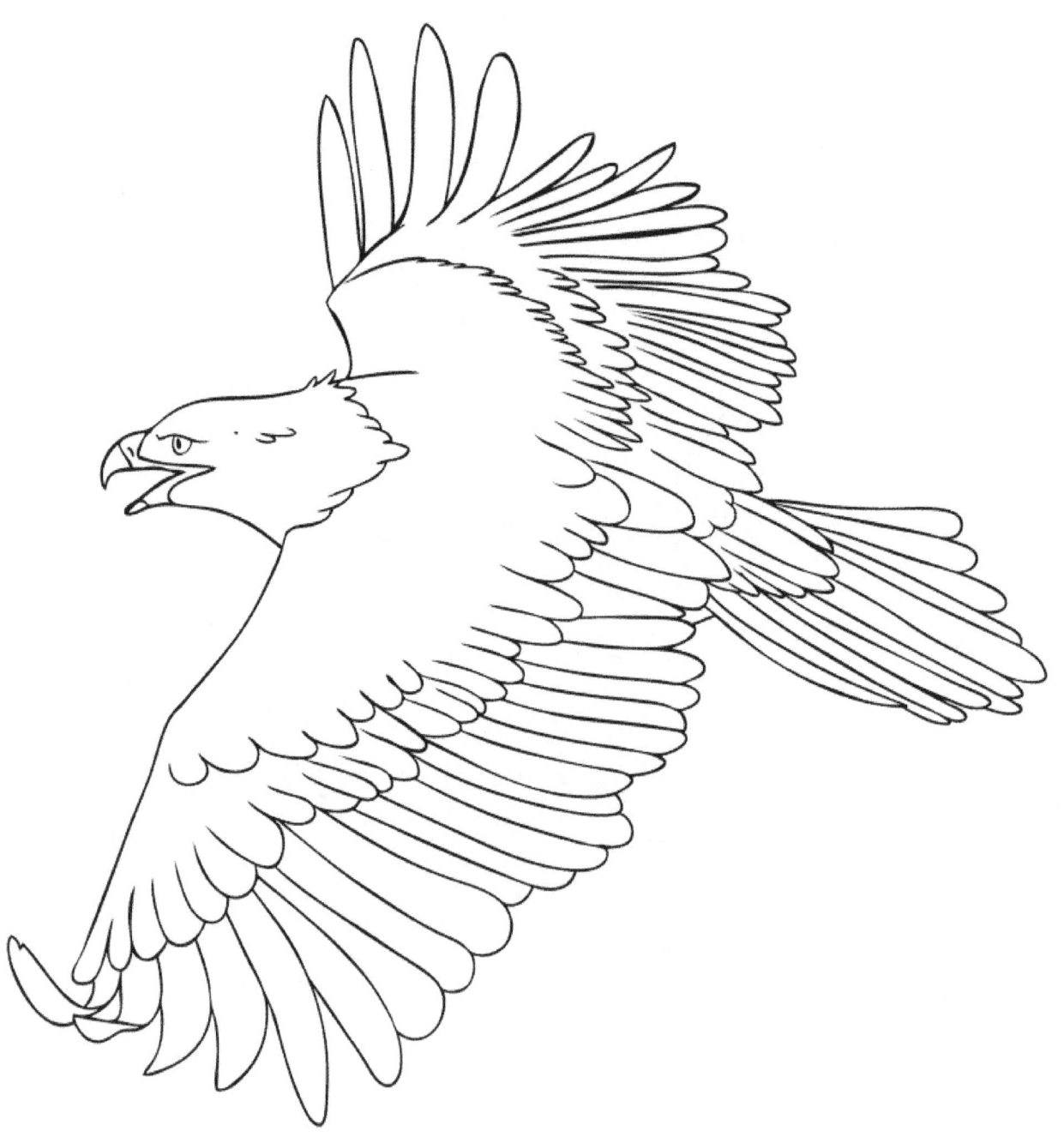

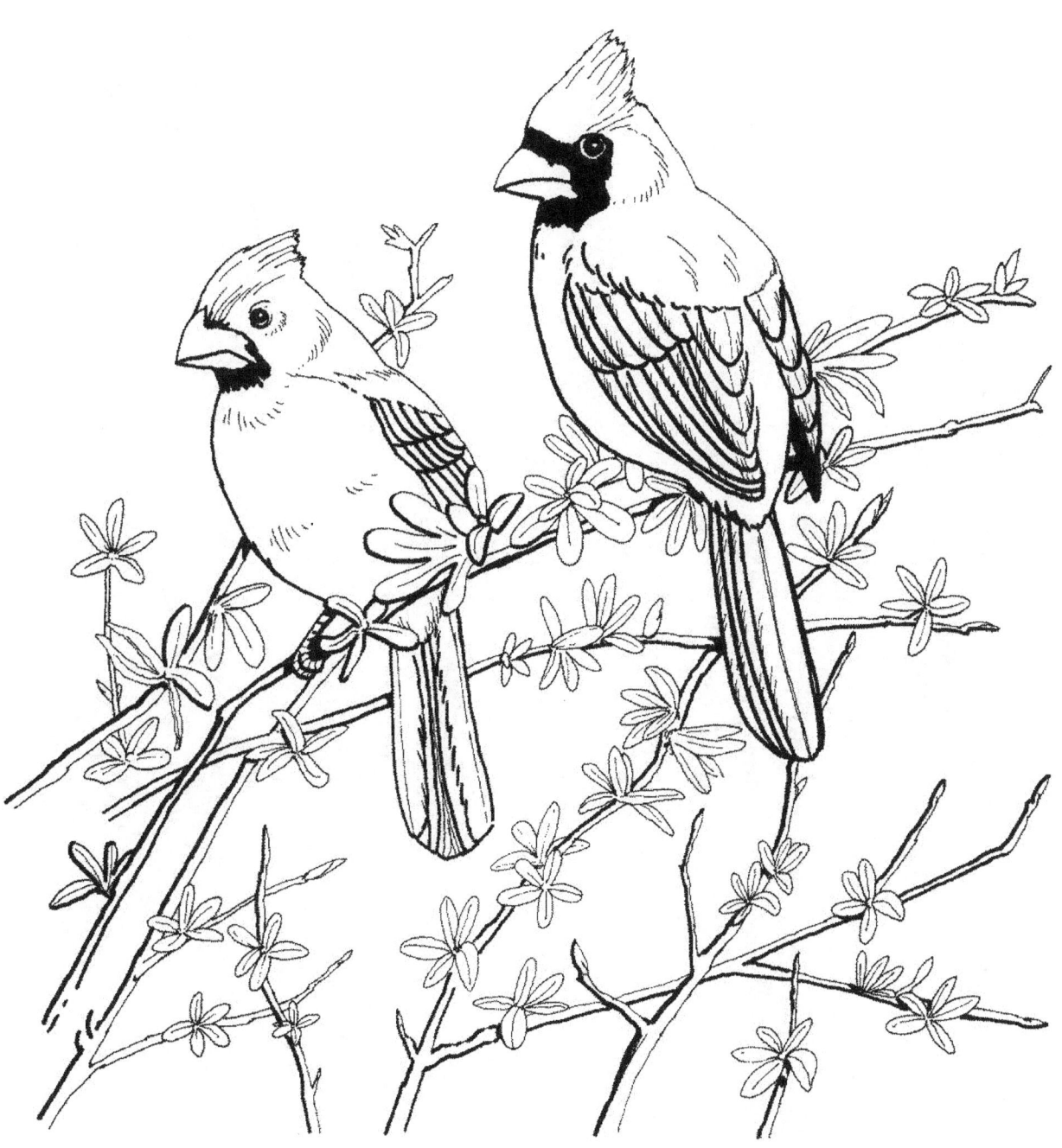

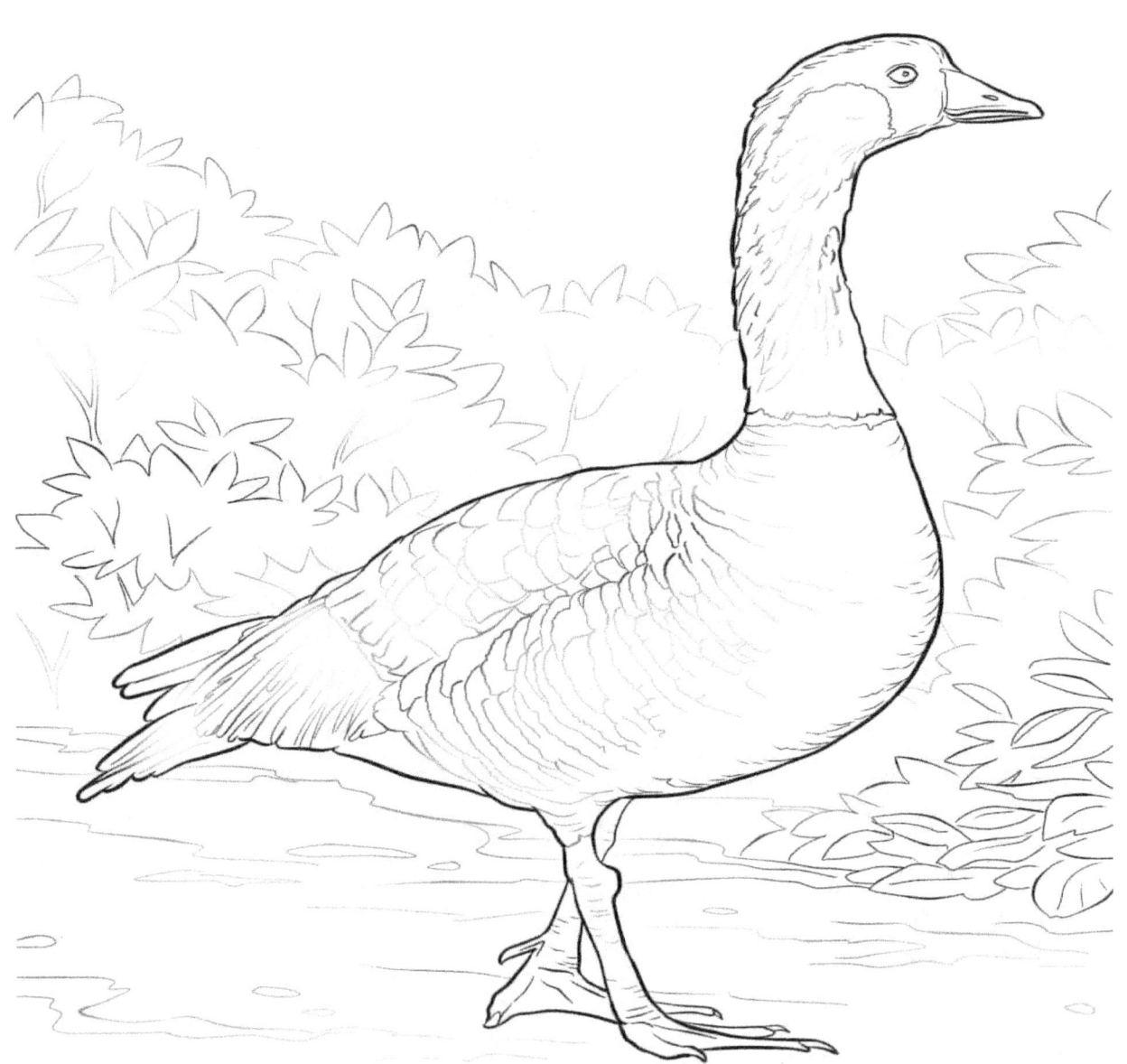

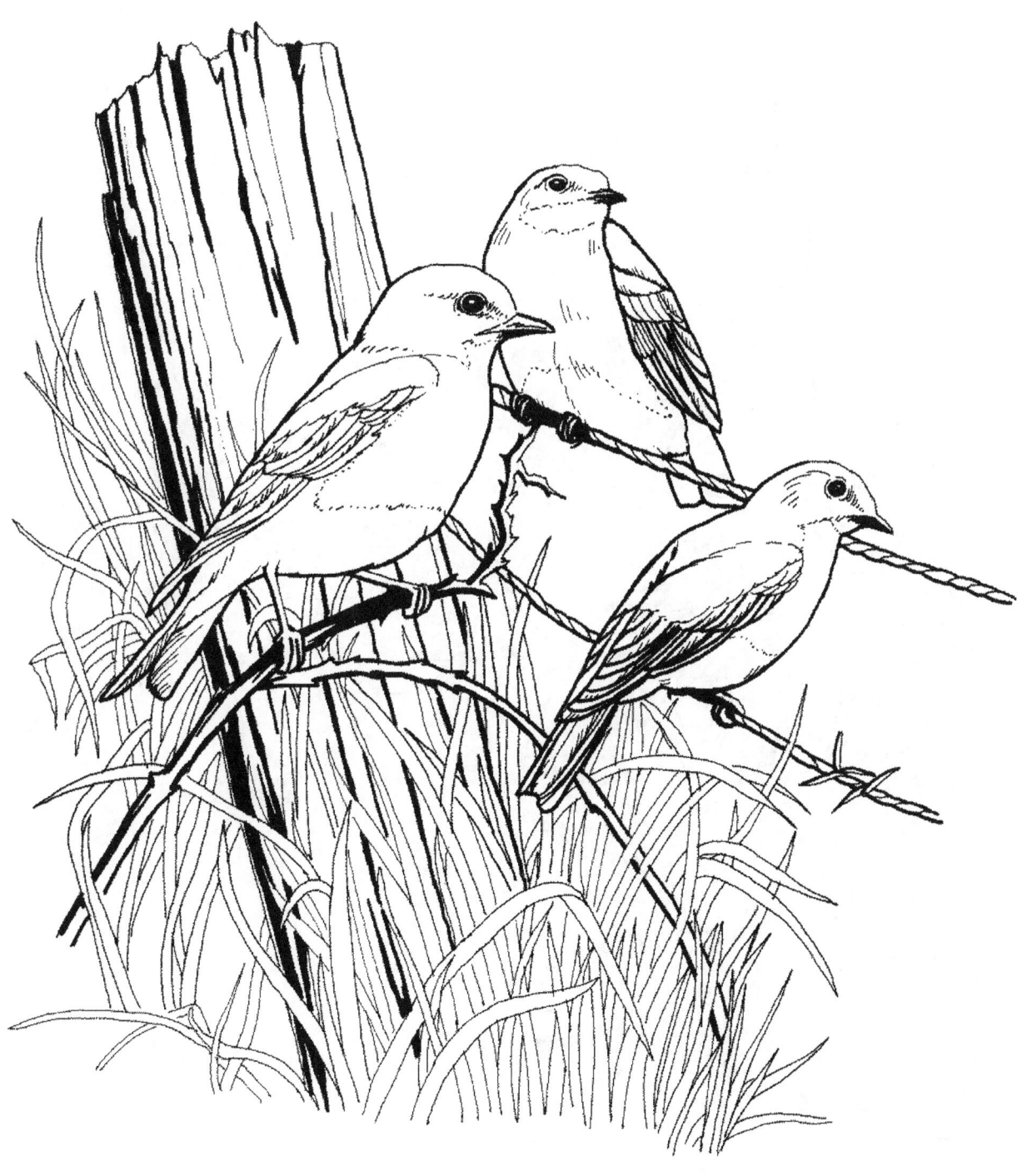

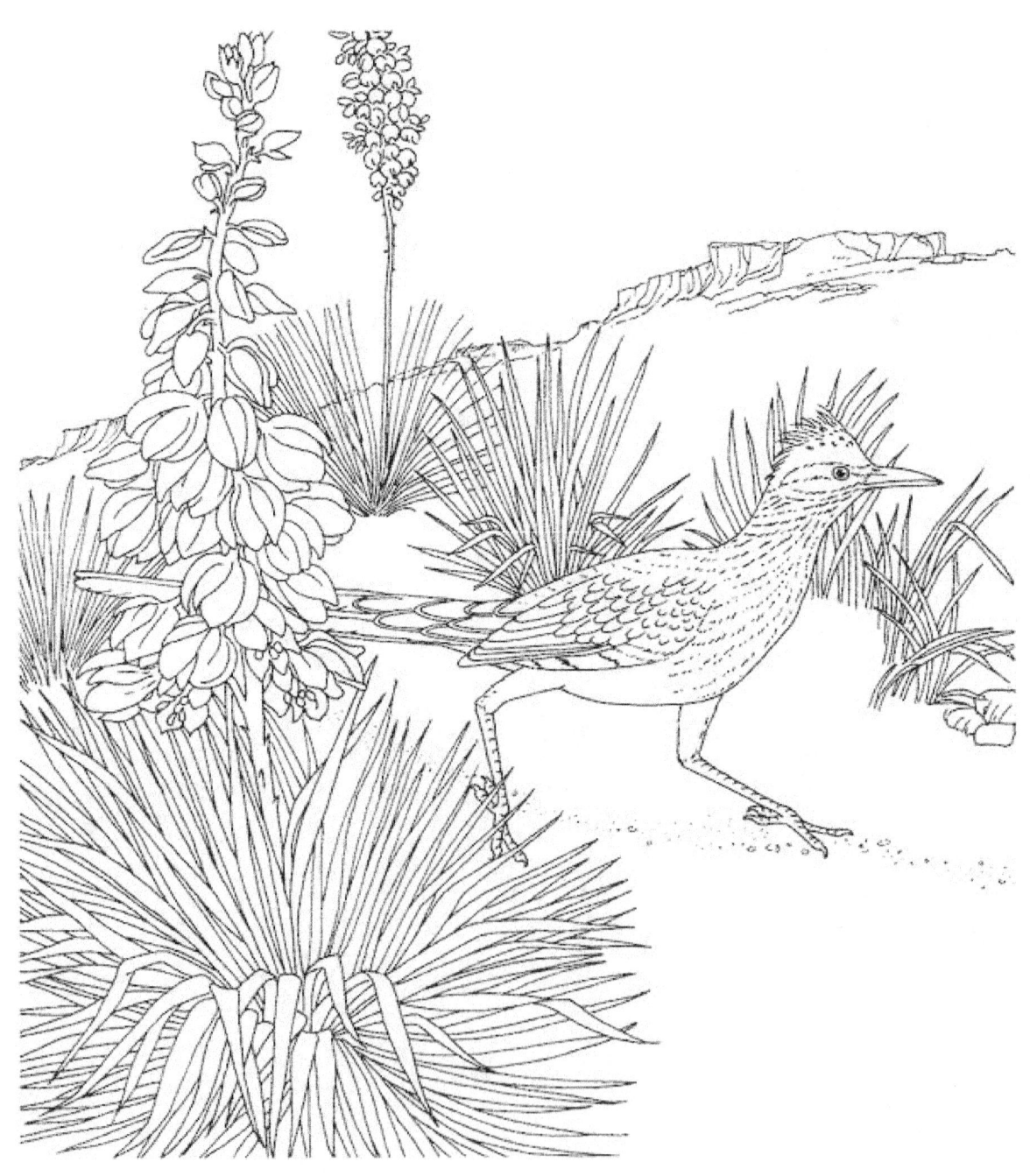

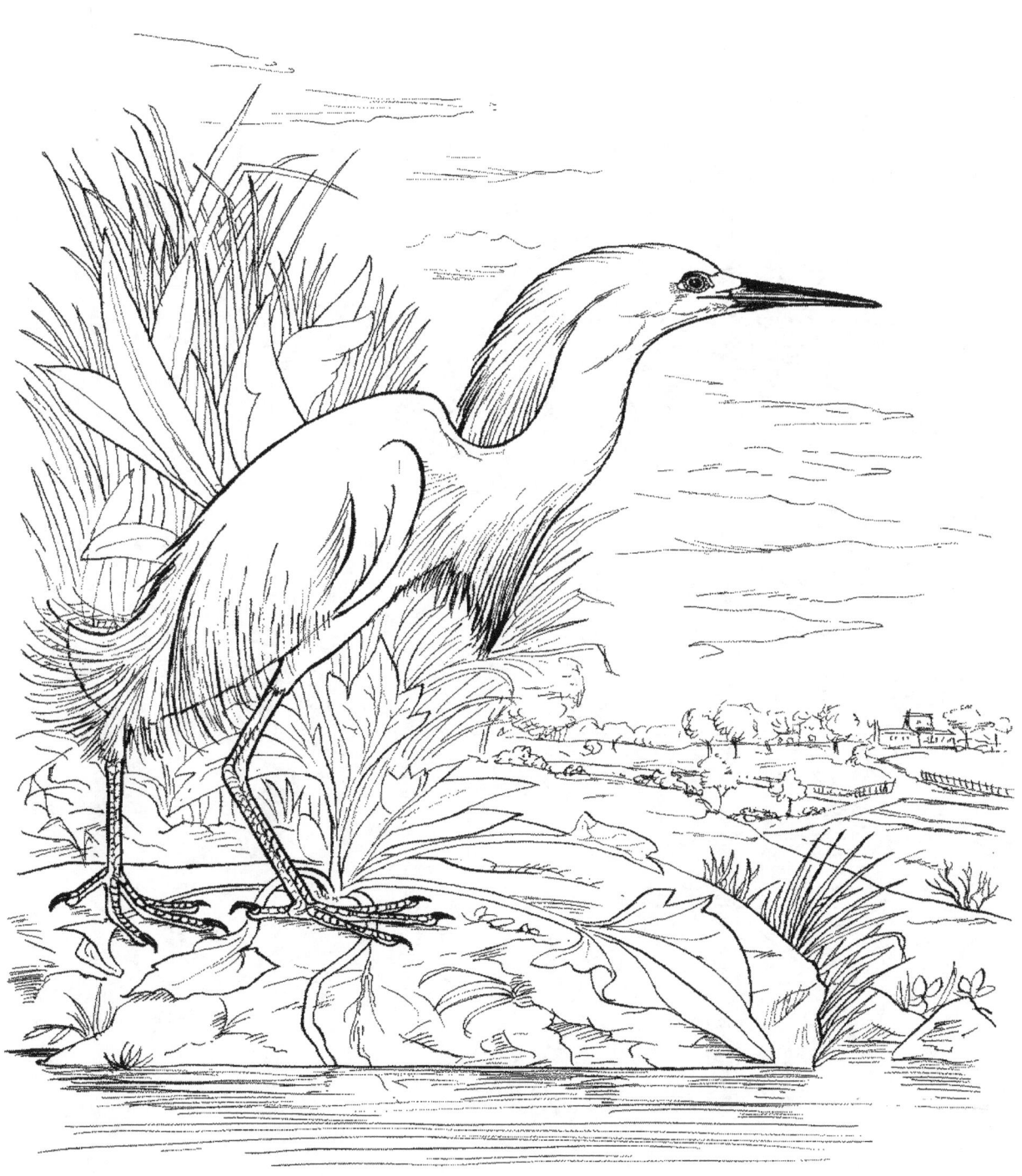

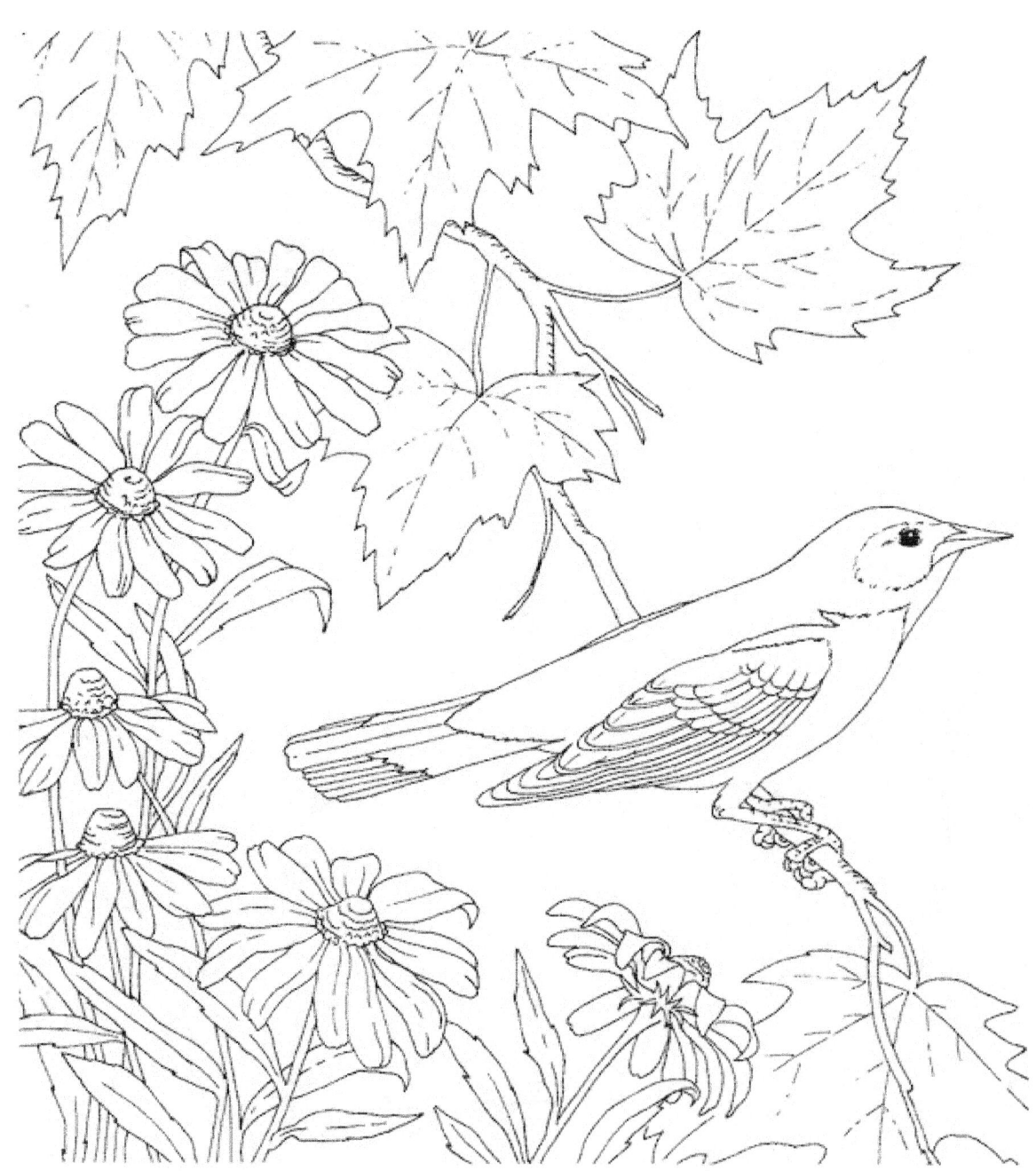

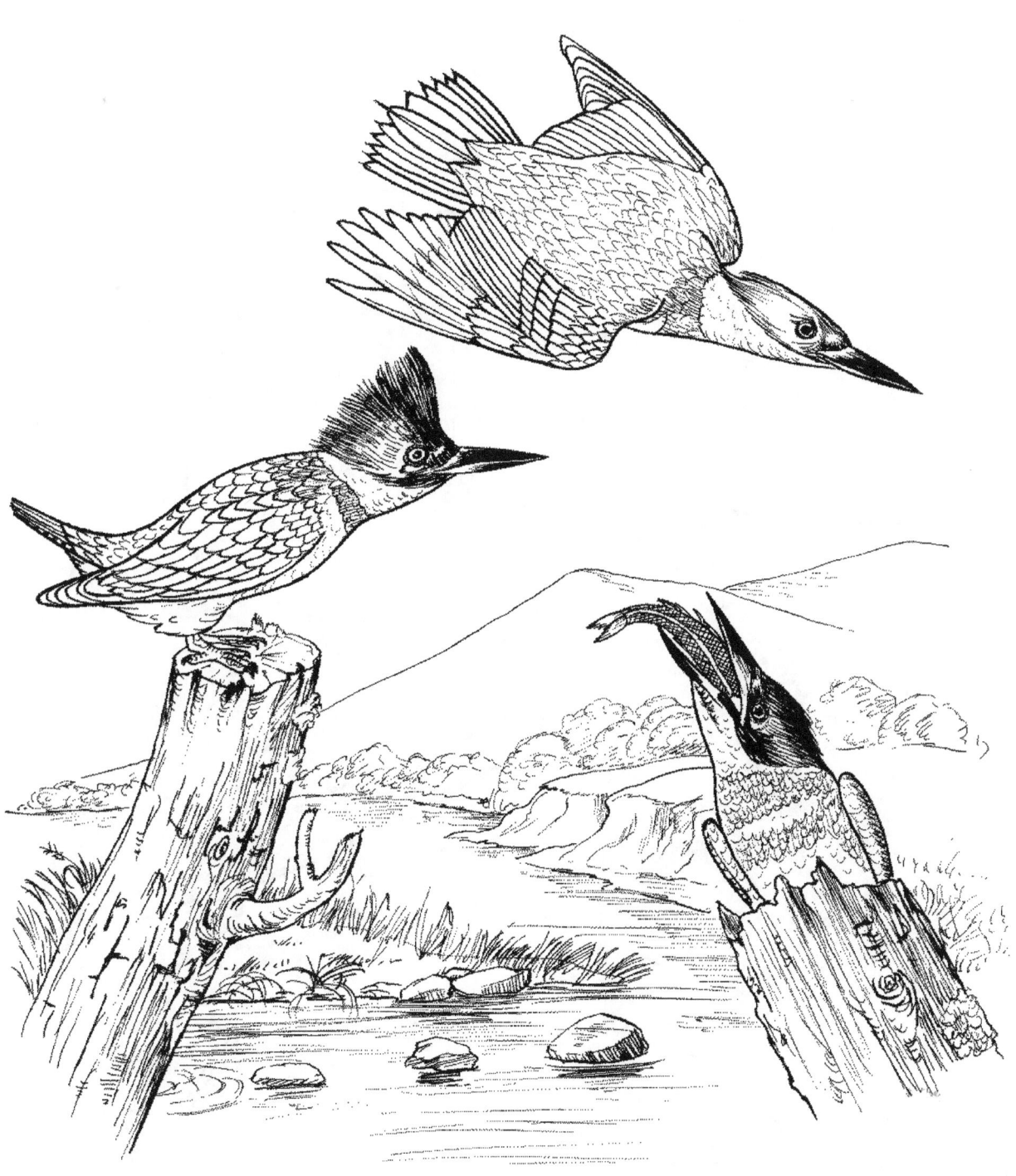

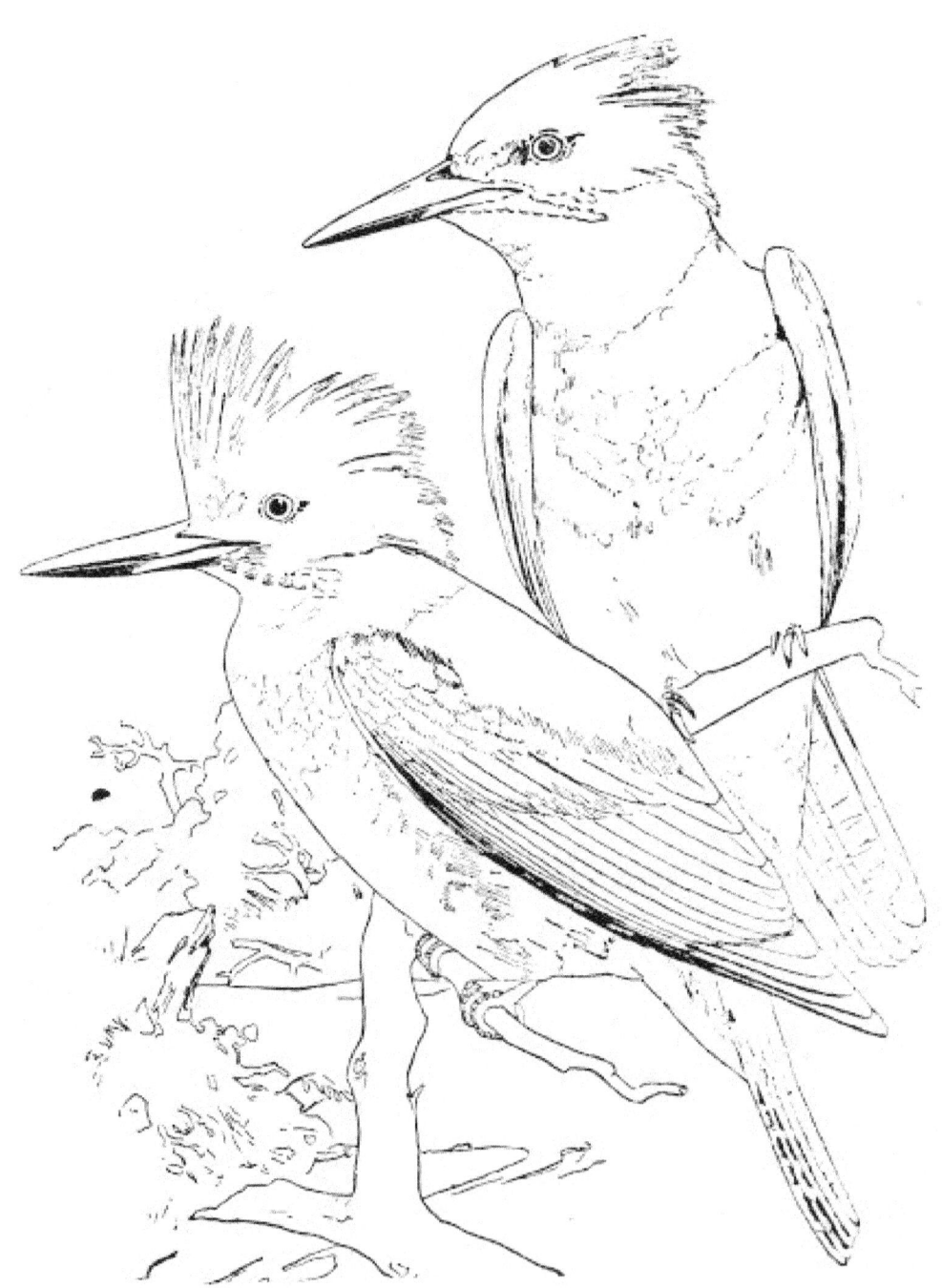

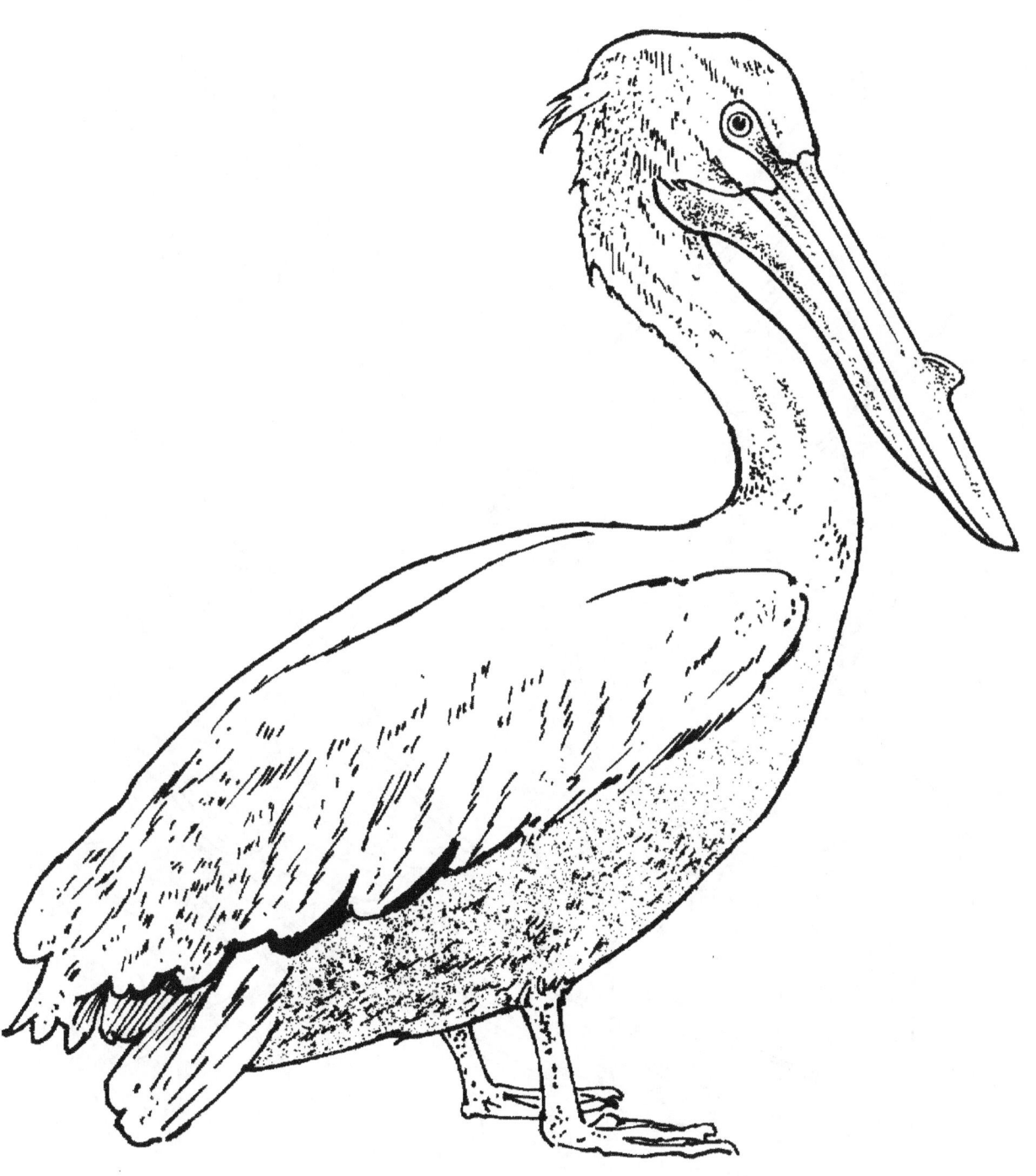

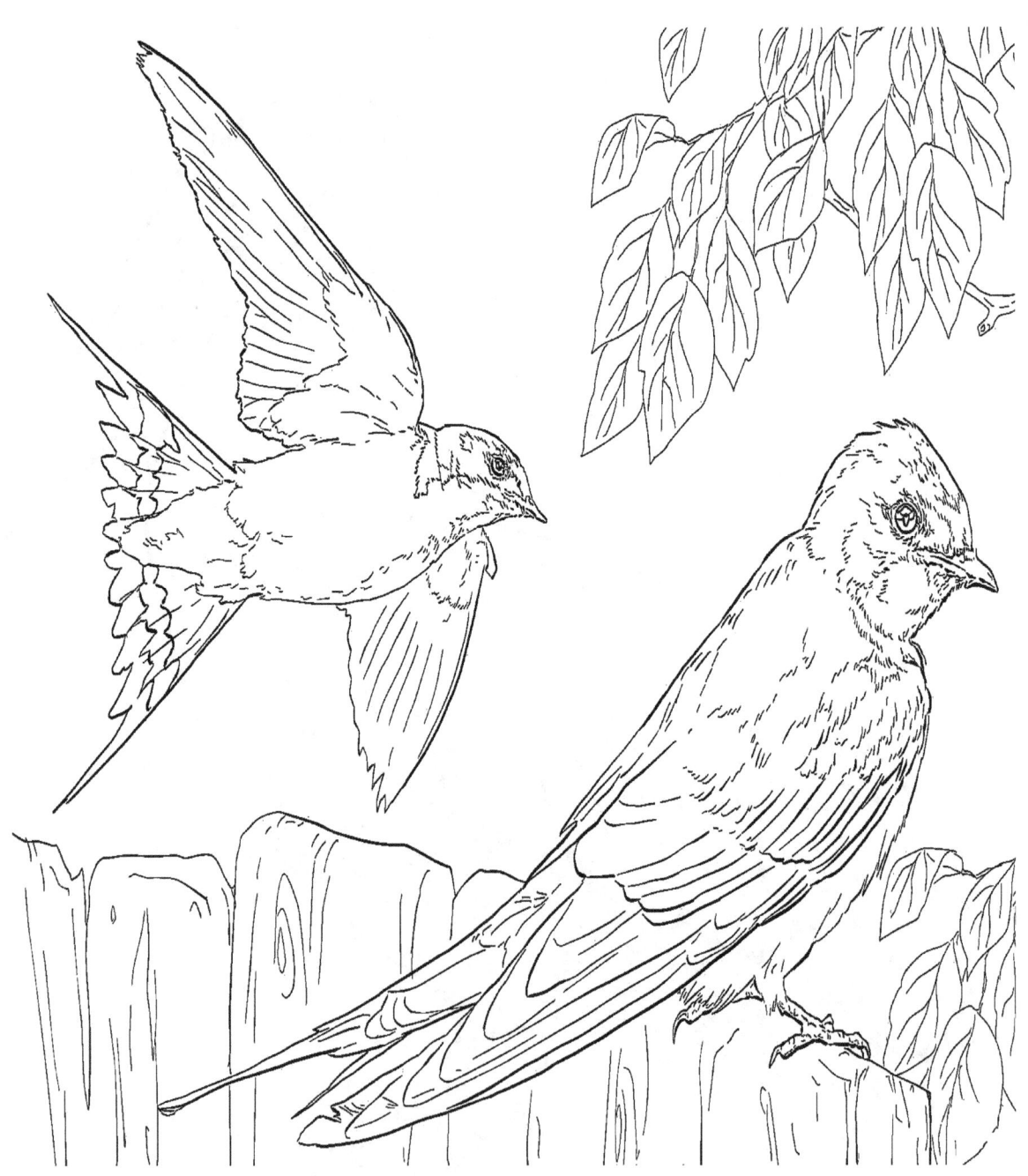

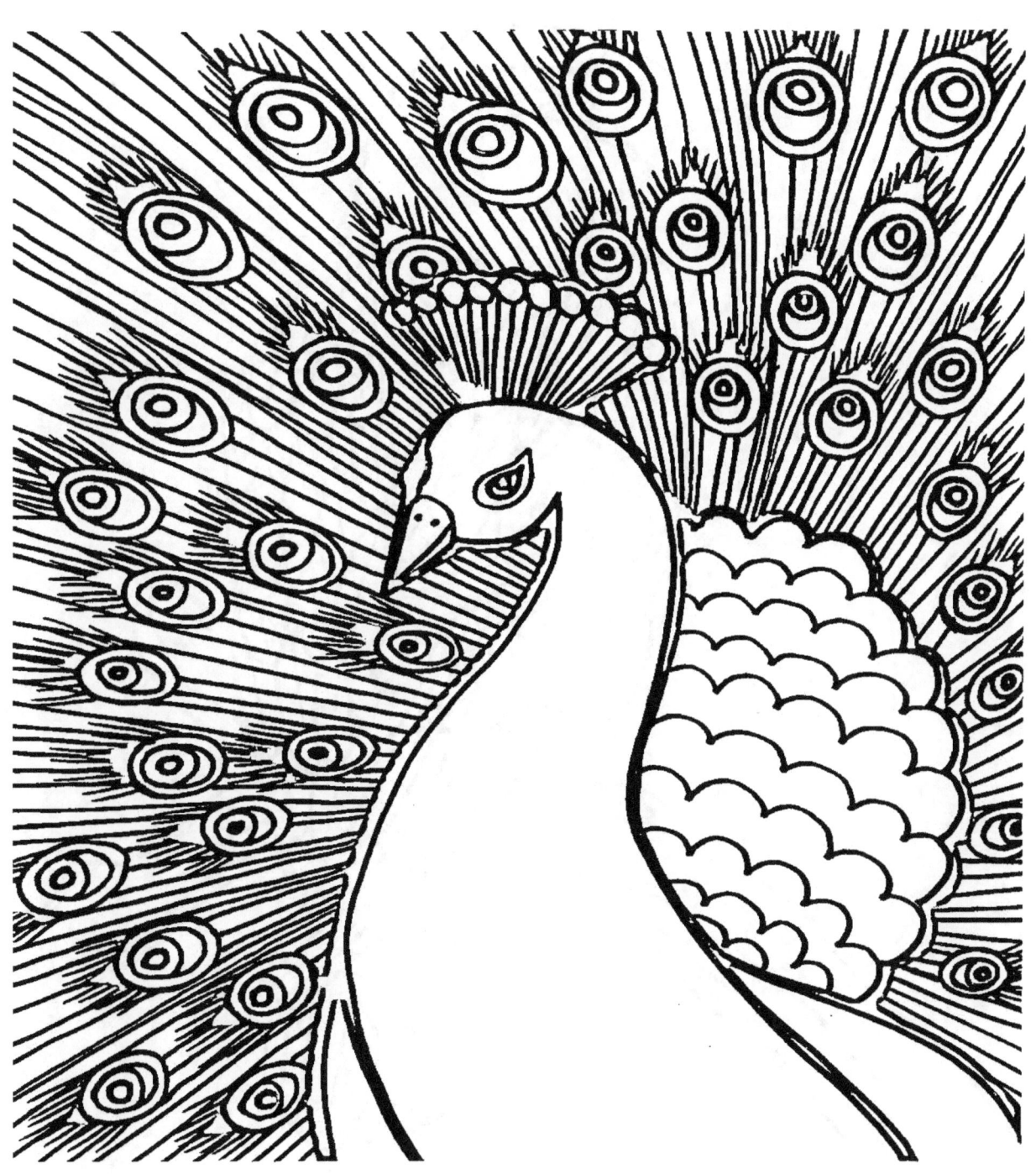

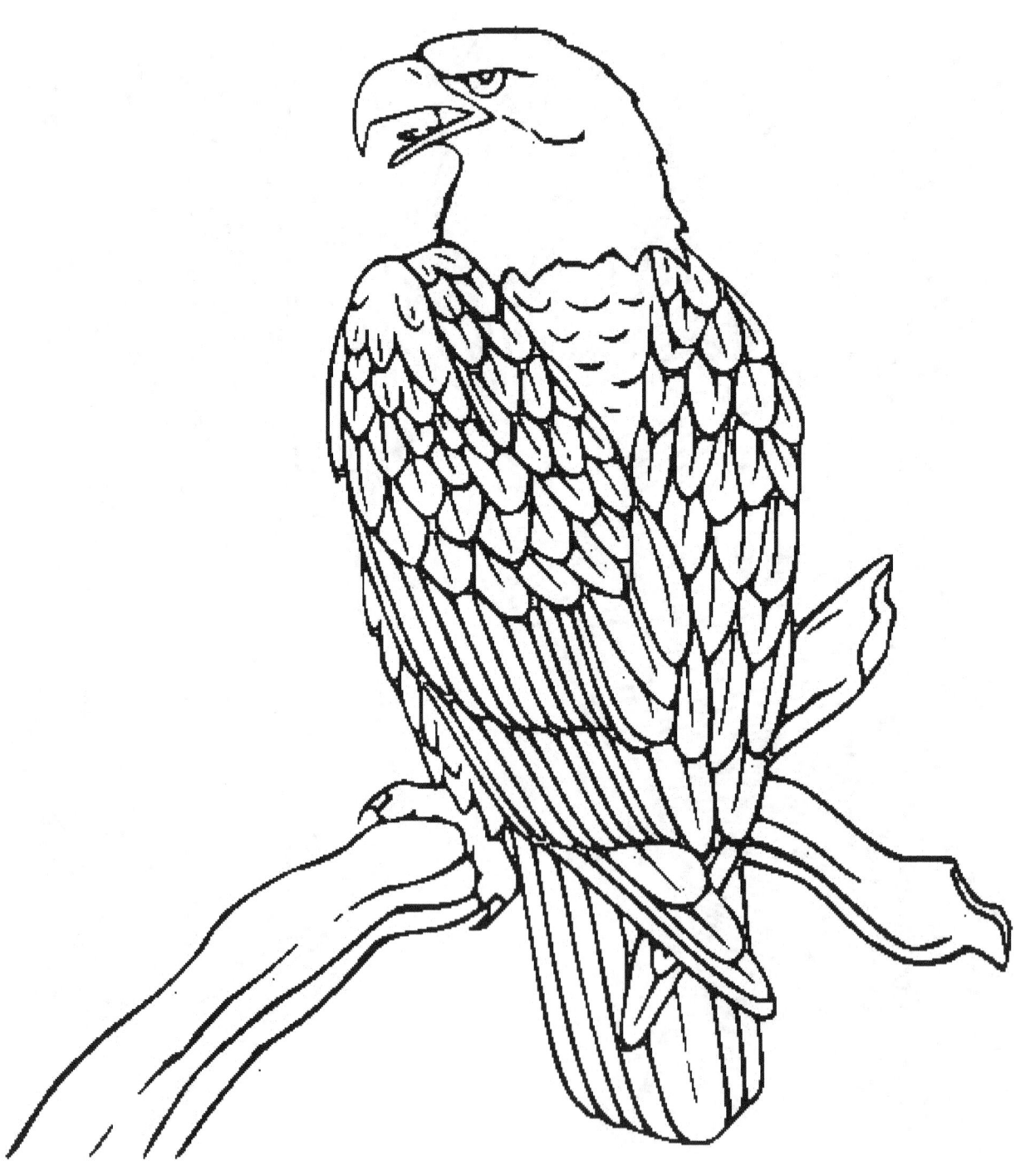

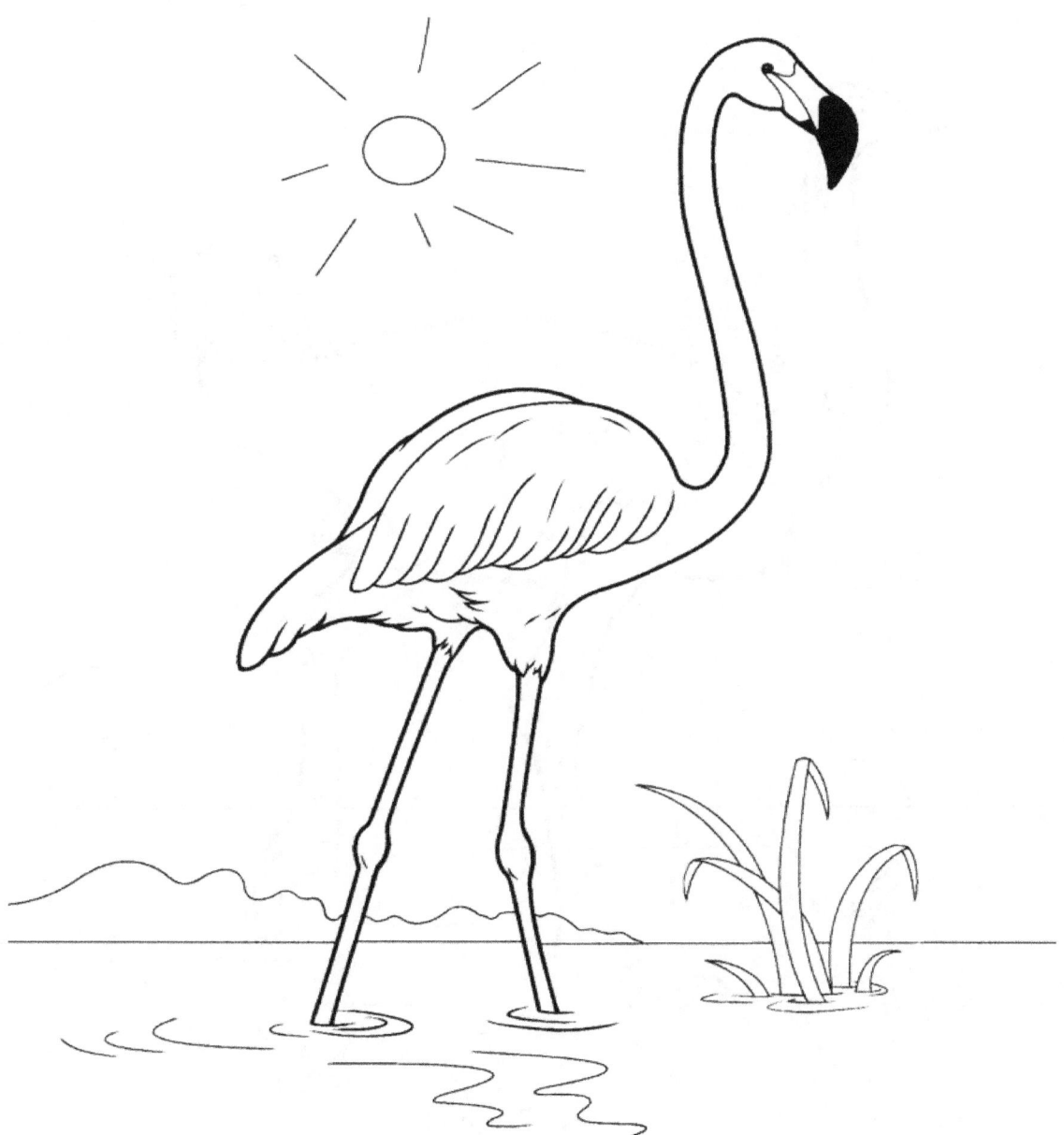

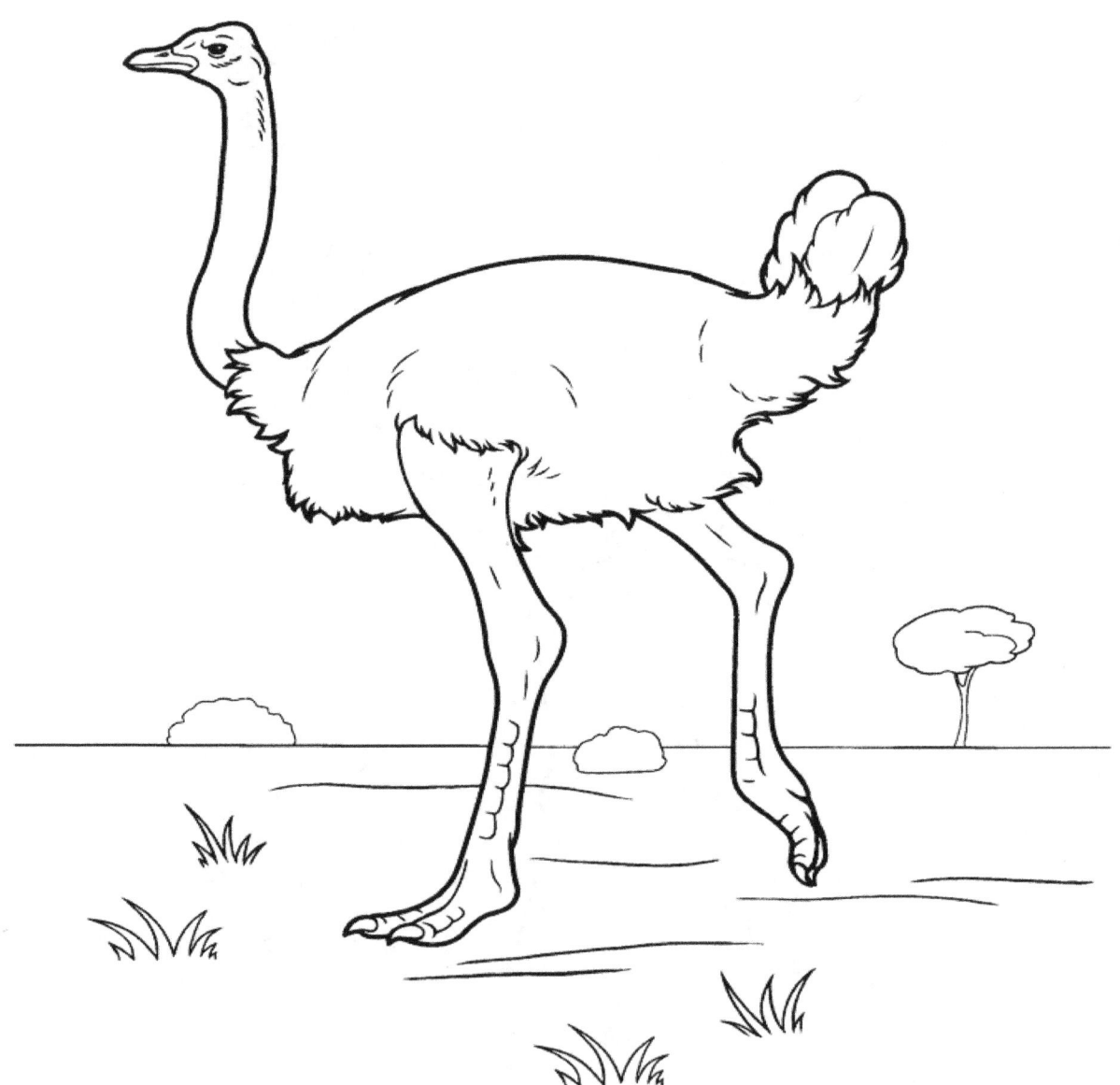

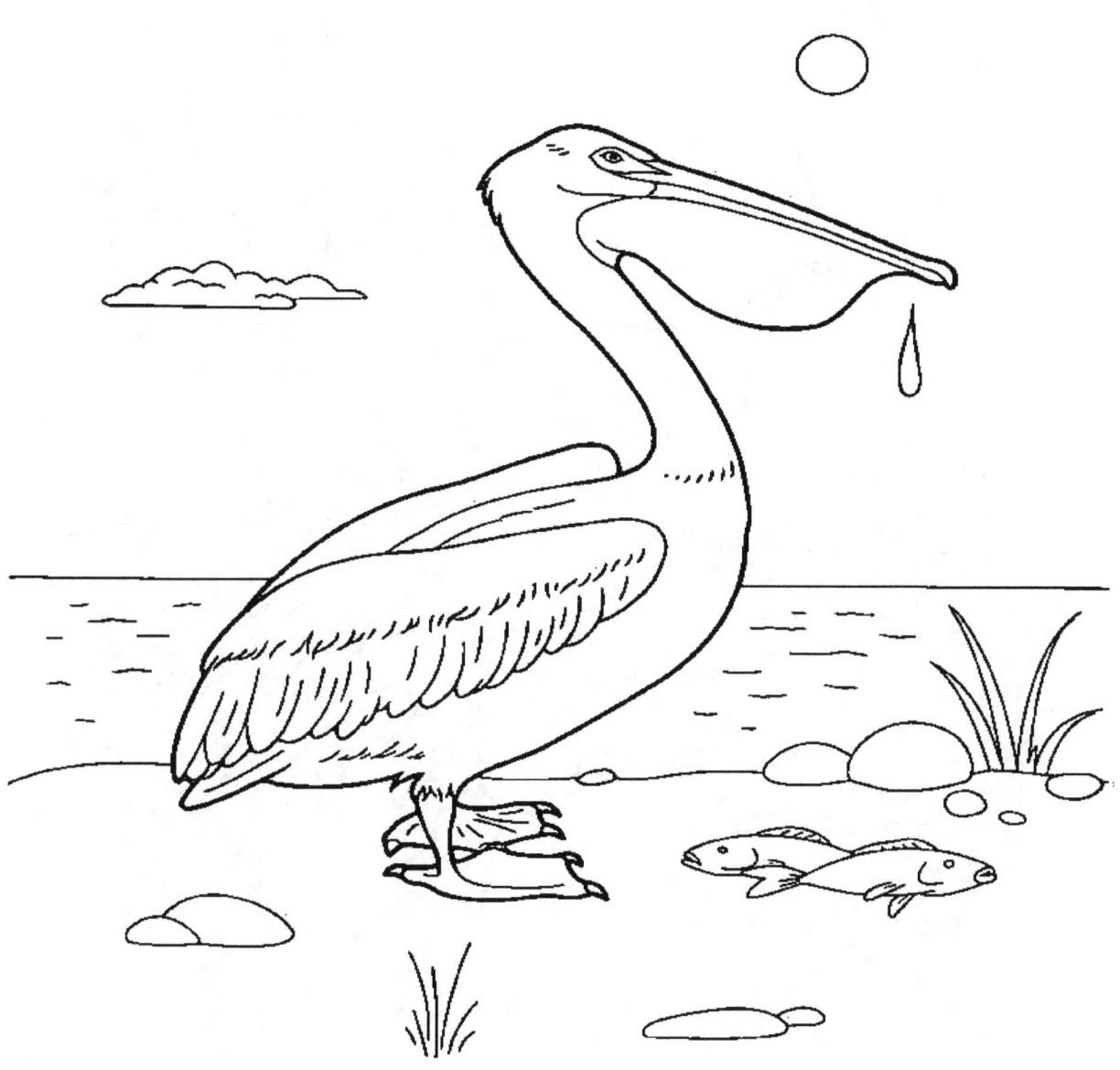

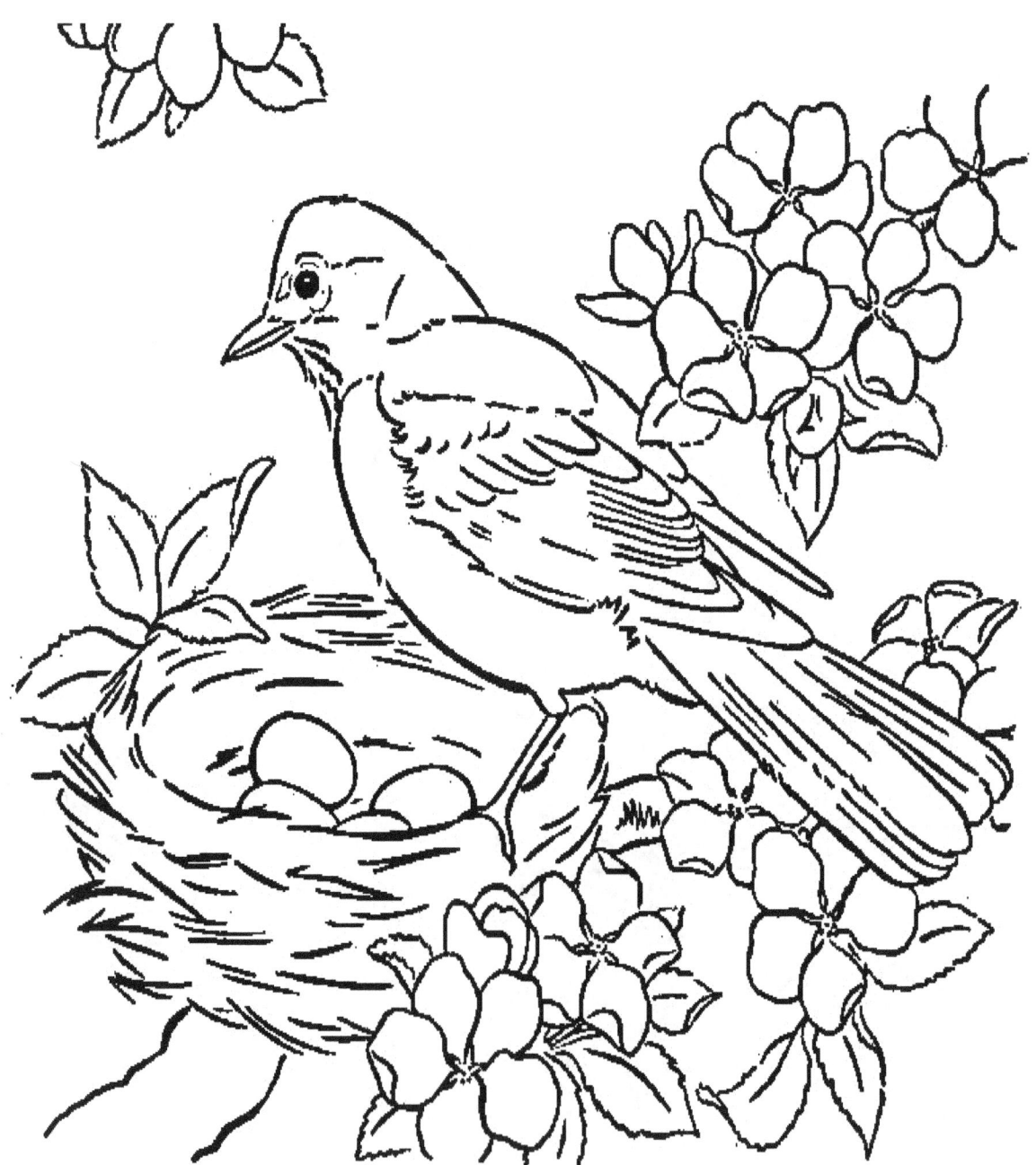

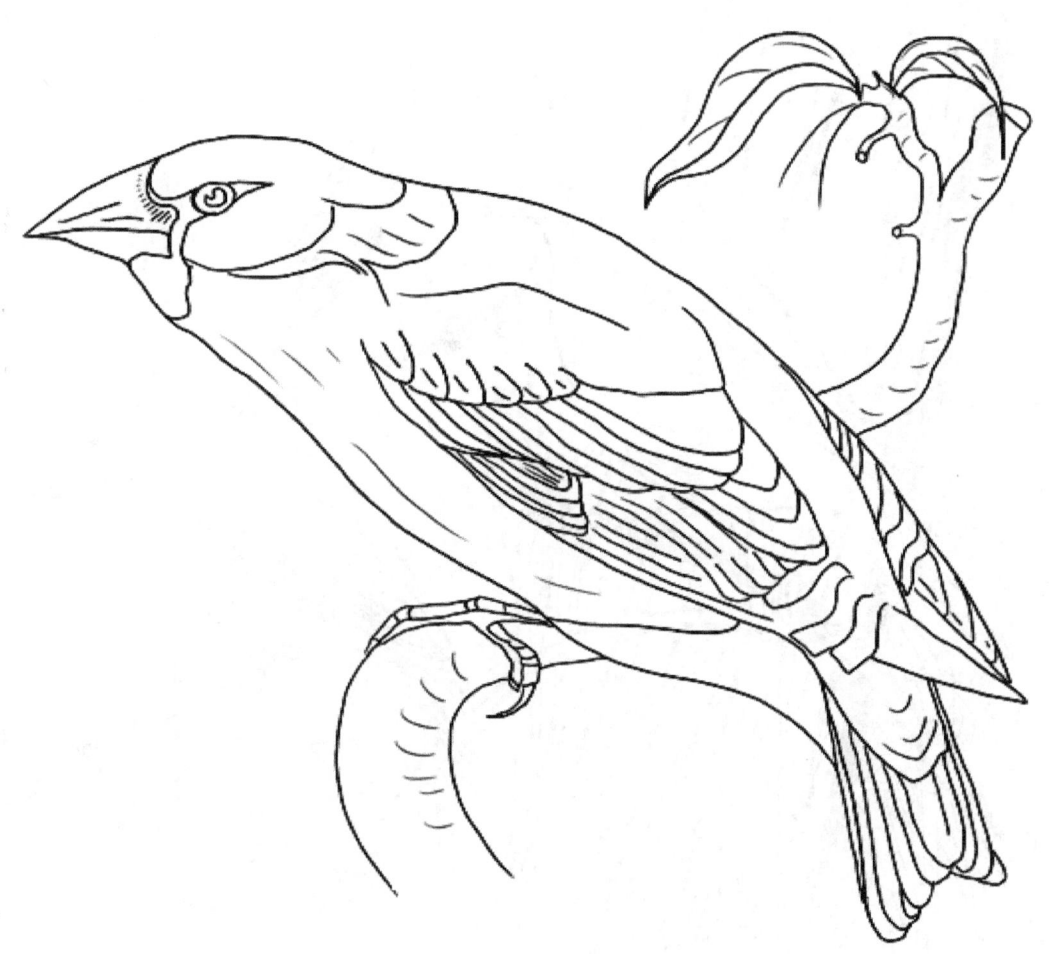

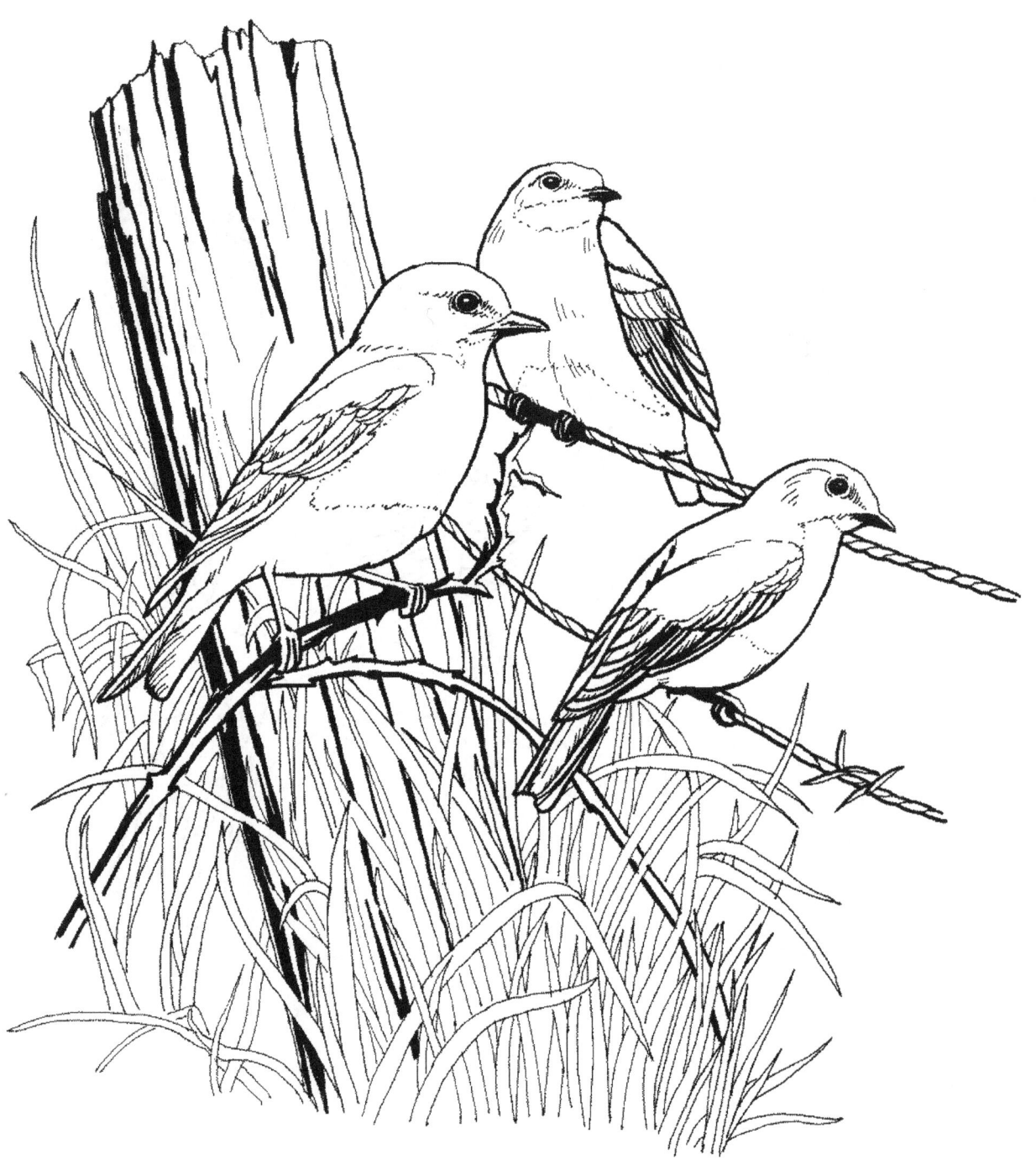

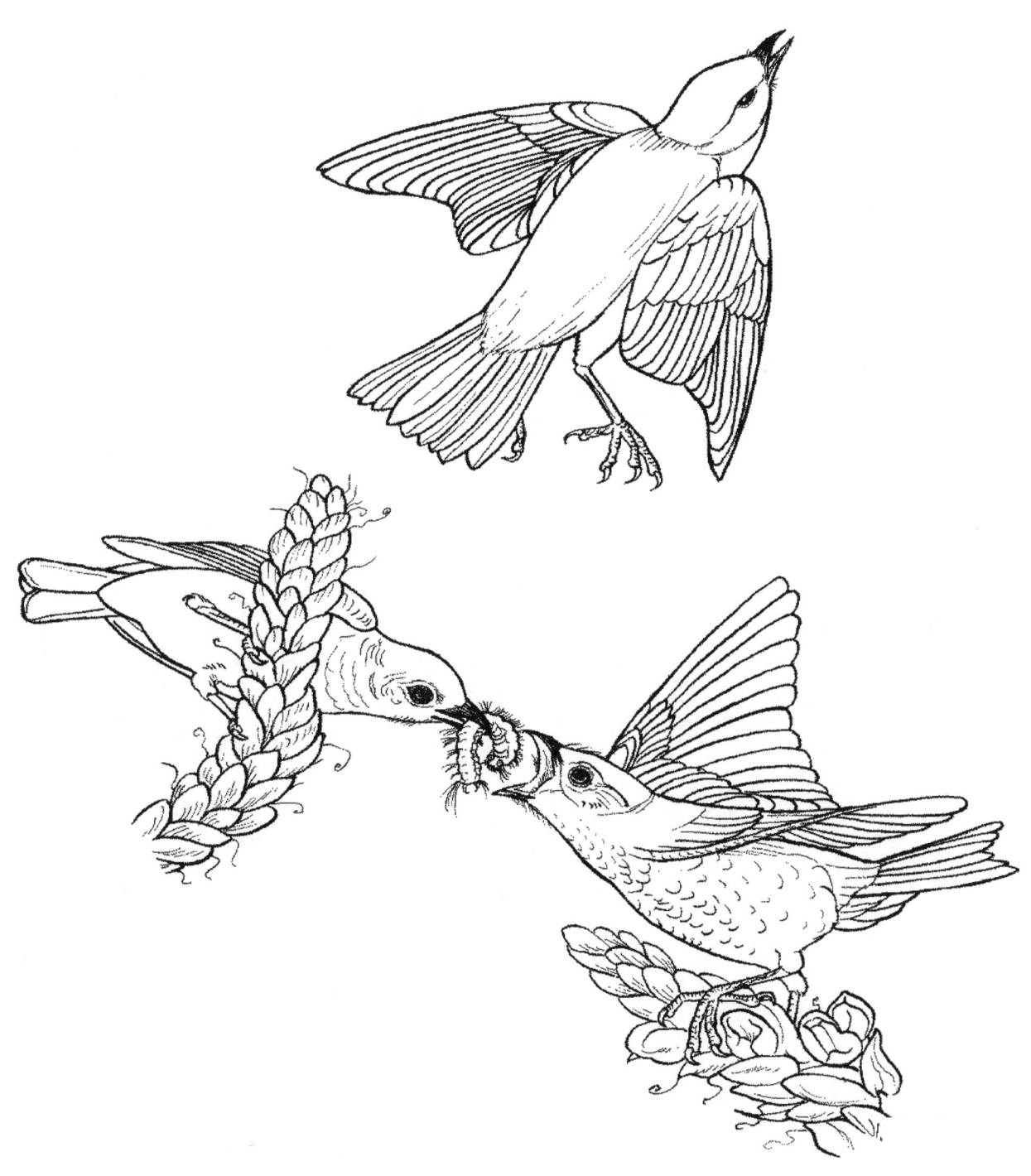